Networks, Open Access, and Virtual Libraries:
Implications for the Research Library

Papers presented at the 1991 Clinic on Library Applications
of Data Processing, April 7-9, 1991
Sponsored by
Graduate School of Library and Information Science
University of Illinois at Urbana-Champaign
and
Committee on Institutional Cooperation

**Clinic on Library Applications
of Data Processing: 1991**

Networks, Open Access, and Virtual Libraries:
Implications for the Research Library

Edited by
BRETT SUTTON
and
CHARLES H. DAVIS

Graduate School of Library and Information Science
University of Illinois at Urbana-Champaign

© 1992 by The Board of Trustees of the University of Illinois
ISBN 0-87845-087-4   ISSN 0069-4789

Printed in the United States of America
on acid-free paper

CONTENTS

Introduction 1
  Brett Sutton

Networked Information: A Revolution in Progress 12
  Clifford A. Lynch

Networked Information Resources and Services:
Next Steps on the Road to the Distributed Digital
Libraries of the Twenty-first Century 40
  Paul Evan Peters

Defining "It": NREN's Opportunities for Librarians 61
  Susan K. Martin

Keeping the Window of Opportunity Open for the
Private Sector 74
  James E. Rush

The Use and Effect of Multimedia Digital Libraries
in a National Network 84
  Charles E. Catlett
  Jeffrey A. Terstriep

Networking Applications for Research Libraries 99
  M. E. L. Jacob

The Changing Economics of Research Libraries 104
  Martin Runkle

The Real Costs and Financial Challenges of Library
Networking: Part 1 118
  Kenneth R. R. Gros Louis

The Real Costs and Financial Challenges of Library
Networking: Part 2 123
  Thomas W. Shaughnessy

Contents *(Cont.)*

**The Real Costs and Financial Challenges of Library
Networking: Part 3** 128
William J. Studer

DRANET: An Information Network 132
Carl R. Grant

**Libraries and Networked Information Systems:
Selected Bibliography** 137
Brett Sutton

Contributors 141

Index 145

Introduction

ELECTRONIC NETWORKS

Networked digital communication is one of the most rapidly maturing technologies in computing. Systems are now in place for conveying electronic messages, documents, and images rapidly and efficiently across long distances; for reaching multiple sites simultaneously; and for linking dissimilar computers interactively in an open communications environment. What is notable about networking is not only the remarkable technology on which it is based but the rapid expansion of its influence. Networked computing was once known mainly to scientists and other specialists fortunate enough to have access to the technology and willing to learn the necessary skills, but that is changing. With costs and administrative barriers to the networks falling, and useful applications and network access points increasing, networked computing is on the verge of entering the mainstream. A principal question for some observers has become not whether digital networks will become as commonplace as the telephone but when. Many other questions remain, however, especially for organizations considering the possibilities of converting from conventional to network processes. Electronic networks pose a variety of operational, economic, and social problems, only some of which have been solved.

Research libraries are among the organizations that are feeling the effects of this convergence of technologies. Not only are innovations in networking likely to transform a variety of traditional library operations (acquisitions, cataloging, interlibrary loan, reference work, resource sharing, and document delivery, to name a few), but they will equip libraries with the tools to create new kinds of services as well.

1

Research librarians are now beginning to ask themselves, with a new sense of urgency, how they might take advantage of this new environment while preserving the best of their traditional roles. These are difficult decisions because development costs are high, support for college and university libraries is already spread too thin, and in spite of progress in the setting of standards there is a great deal of movement and instability in the technical environment.

Whether these new circumstances constitute a crisis or an opportunity depends partly on local conditions. Some libraries, especially those with plentiful resources, an administrative taste for experimental system development, and key staff members to take leadership roles, have been successful in adapting the emerging network technologies to fit existing services and devising new services specifically for the networked environment. Other libraries with less flexibility and fewer resources have proceeded more cautiously, opting for fewer immediate benefits in exchange for fewer risks. At stake is not just the operational issue of how research libraries will do their jobs but the changing role of the research library itself. Not everyone involved is convinced that progress towards the networked library is compatible with the research library's established academic identity and purpose. For some observers, the research library is too bound to its historic mission of storing and organizing printed materials, too well adapted to its traditional niche and unable to evolve quickly enough, and will have to adjust to a diminished role in the future if it survives the transition at all. But other observers see the research library as an organic, adaptive institution, capable of riding the forces of change to emerge as a leader in networked information services. A unified vision for the research library of the future does not yet exist.

Coming to terms with the consequences of library networking, and contributing to its realization, is the collective task of everyone who has a role in the future of the research library. The essays in this volume are part of that effort. The writers, who address a range of issues in computer networking and its application in research libraries, include academic library directors, system developers and administrators, members of the scientific computing community, library consultants, and university administrators. Some are technical authorities, but many are not. The diversity of the expertise they bring to the question of higher education, research, and networked information systems is as varied as the conclusions they have drawn. Collectively they present a realistic picture of the adaptive processes that are taking place at the intersection of the research library and advanced computer networking.

THE ORIGINS OF LIBRARY NETWORKING

The emergence of the network model of digital communication and its adoption by the library community cannot be traced to any single event or organization but has developed along several fronts simultaneously. One of the first networking systems to become widely used in colleges and universities was BITNET, a mainframe-based messaging and file transfer system. Besides taking advantage of the electronic mail services of BITNET, academic librarians have used BITNET's LISTSERV software to establish a number of computer conferences devoted to library topics. The scientific community, working in conjunction with the government and the computing and telecommunications industries, have fostered the development of other networks, including ARPANET, established under the auspices of the Advanced Research Project Agency of the Department of Defense, and its successor, NSFNET. These systems, faster and more interactive than BITNET, have evolved into what is now known as the Internet, the global network of networks that has become the most direct means for interconnecting the educational, research, and library communities. The Internet is the model and inspiration for the more powerful and inclusive networking systems that are still in the planning stages.

Although the academic community has carried much of the responsibility for creating these networks, government has played a critical role, both administratively and financially. The seriousness of the federal commitment to the national network has been manifested most recently by the *High-Performance Computing Act of 1991*. This legislation, championed by Senator Albert Gore, will establish the National Research and Education Network (NREN), an administrative structure designed to promote the continued development of the national computer network, which will in turn support development projects in both education and industry. Constituting the primary links in this network is the national "backbone," a set of fiber-optic trunk lines operated by the National Science Foundation. This backbone, already in place but constantly being upgraded, provides fast long-distance data transmission services to various regional, state, and organizational networks, which in turn extend network access to their own communities. The capacity of this network for moving data, projected to reach 3 billion bits per second before the end of the decade, has suggested the operating metaphor of a "superhighway," analogous to the federal interstate highway system begun in the 1950s. Although these electronic highways are constructed of fast transmission lines and advanced processing machines rather than asphalt and concrete, the analogy is a useful one. Like the federal highway system, the network is planned to be a public resource, established with public funds, constructed by commercial contractors, and made freely available to a wide variety of users at many different levels. Advocates of library networking have recognized that the NREN's primary roles, facilitating educational communication and disseminating information, are also the primary roles of the academic library, and they believe that the network represents a golden opportunity for libraries to lend their expertise to the effort of developing a productive new research environment.

Although the excitement over the Internet is the most immediate source of librarians' interest in networking, shared access to remote computers is an idea that is well established in the library community. Like many other public and private organizations, libraries have practiced their own forms of networking for many years. Since the development of the first automated systems, libraries have found ways to provide enhanced electronic access to their holdings, beginning with locally designed, mainframe-based circulation systems in the 1960s, which were succeeded by the efficient turnkey systems of the 1970s, and more recently by hybrid systems taking advantage of small but ubiquitous and increasingly interconnected microcomputers in the 1980s. The introduction of the MARC (machine-readable cataloging) record and other standards helped to launch OCLC, RLIN, and numerous regional library networks dedicated to the sharing of cataloging and authority records and other automated services. These developments helped make possible collaborative automation efforts in which a single system could provide collective access to the holdings of cooperating libraries, facilitating resource sharing that benefited libraries both small and large.

The success of automated systems has fostered the development of numerous new features: online public access catalogs supporting enhanced searching techniques, supplementary bibliographic databases mounted alongside the public access catalog, CD-ROMs mounted on local area networks. At many sites, these library resources have been linked to other information utilities in campuswide networked information systems, and some have even been opened up to remote users over wide area networks. Librarians are also users of other kinds of networks, including the commercial packet switching services that provide access to remote commercial database providers such as DIALOG and BRS, direct lines to book jobbers, and networks established by vendors of automated library systems for their clients. The Internet has already begun to absorb some of the traffic generated by these applications. The point is that when libraries compare the new networks with their own operations, their standard of comparison is not manual operations, but a well developed, though more localized and controlled, form of networking.

Finally, it is worth noting that the inspiration for networking has not come exclusively from institutional sources, whether government, industry, or the universities. Much of the creative energy that has gone into the development of network resources has come not from formal organizations at all but from self-educated experimenters working locally in less-structured environments. Individual users working on multiuser machines, or even on microcomputers equipped with inexpensive modems, have created, with very little central planning or supervision, a highly distributed, decentralized, grass roots kind of telecomputing that has helped pave the way for more institutionalized networks. It is these users, enthusiastically embracing the concept of "cyberspace" and pioneering computer conferences and bulletin boards in networks such as USENET, FIDONET, and more recently the WELL, that are now calling for the democratization of the networks and the removal of barriers separating the public from the powerful networks that well-placed academicians take for granted. It is not without significance that these values of open access and cooperation are also basic to the traditional library ethic.

NETWORK APPLICATIONS IN LIBRARIES

The national network is essentially a communication system that constitutes an environment for performing certain tasks, but it does not specify what those tasks should be. Like the computer itself, it is a multipurpose tool that can be adapted to serve a diverse range of activities. One of the main tasks for libraries, in fact, is to invent interesting new uses for this powerful resource. The Internet has already been the setting for a variety of experiments in information dissemination potentially useful to the library community, only some of which have been created in library settings. These experiments are the early stages of a development process that will eventually yield new multimedia communication systems, new forms of electronic publishing, transmission that will be for practical purposes instantaneous, and direct access to data collections larger than many sites could store locally. Many leaders in the library community believe that research libraries, because of their long experience in organizing information, should take a leadership role in developing these new network applications. Several contributors to this volume, particularly Clifford Lynch and Paul Peters, discuss in some detail the potential of library networking in this environment.

Although predicting how network applications will eventually unfold is difficult, it is possible to identify from current practice the various sorts of functions that are most likely to receive attention in the future. Among the simplest and most widely used network features are electronic mail and file transfer between individuals. In libraries, these tools can serve not only as a medium for maintaining professional contacts, but these tools have potential in collaborative reference work and the delivery of search results to patrons. Extended to public bulletin board and conferencing environments, these applications make it possible for special interest groups to carry on open discussions with unprecedented immediacy and efficiency. With some additional development, these basic communications tools will make it possible for a wide variety of more formal library business transactions, such as book ordering and interlibrary loan requests, to be handled in the paper-free environment of the network.

Another promising area of network development is direct electronic access to library resources across institutional boundaries. Many research libraries, having created in-house online public access catalogs (OPACs), have taken additional steps to make them available to local users via dialup lines, and more broadly to remote users over the Internet. Although it is true that the primary clients of remote library catalogs are professional staff and others with Internet skills and access privileges, some libraries have begun to build within their own public access systems bridges to selected remote systems as a service to all users. For example, at this writing, users of the University of California's MELVYL system have access, if they want it, to university library catalogs in Colorado, New Mexico, Tennessee, Massachusetts, and several other states. One problem is that users of remote systems, for the time being anyway, must learn to use each system and the peculiarities of its interface separately—a rather daunting prospect for those who may not even know their home systems very well. The implementation of standards such as the Z39.50 protocols for information retrieval may eventually provide for more transparent remote access, but at this stage using remote systems requires patience and practice.

Online library catalogs are no longer restricted to being electronic versions of the card catalog but are becoming multidimensional information systems. Many research libraries now provide access for local users to supplementary databases of journal literature from commercial sources such as Wilson or DIALOG. These resources are usually subject to license restrictions that permit access to local users only. Remote users are becoming familiar with the frustration of seeing them listed on the OPAC's opening menu, only to find they have no access privileges. Some libraries, however, have developed their own supplementary databases that are not restricted and are freely available to guest users from outside the community. Such systems, developed locally but designed for open network access, are already common in the scientific community. Charles Catlett and Jeffrey Terstriep of the

National Center for Supercomputing Applications describe in this volume research that will lead to the development of "digital libraries" for the storage and network dissemination of scientific data. Some libraries, too, have established interesting and useful resources that are accessible via the Internet, such as Dartmouth's full-text Shakespeare database and CARL's collection of book reviews from *Choice.* At some sites, the online library resources are part of comprehensive campus information systems offering information on campus events, faculty directories, course schedules, bookstore inventories, and other useful topics. Other systems, such as the Cleveland FreeNet, are public systems serving the entire community.

Still in the experimental stages, but potentially capable of radically altering the way research results are disseminated, is the electronic journal. Whether peer reviewed or not, free or fee based, issued regularly or irregularly, these network-distributed sources of scholarly writing enjoy several advantages over their printed counterparts, particularly in the speed with which research results can be made available to a community of interested scholars. A number of issues remain unresolved. For the research community, details relating to peer review, credit for promotion and tenure, copyright, and cost recovery have yet to be worked out. For libraries, the challenges include solving the unique acquisitions, storage, and public access problems presented by electronic publications. Also unresolved is the very form such journals will take. Most of the existing journals are distributed as simple text files, similar in form to standard electronic mail, but there is some interest in providing more sophisticated formats. An example is the recently announced electronic publication, the *Online Journal of Current Clinical Trials,* produced jointly by the American Association for the Advancement of Science and OCLC. This publication will be distributed in a graphics format permitting, with the use of appropriate software, the display of illustrations and typeset-quality printing. Such journals, if successful, could become an important new source of scholarly information, and libraries will have to find ways to access and manage them.

The presence on the network of electronic archives containing documents, directories, back issues of electronic journals and newsletters, and even software, all available for copying across the network, constitutes another potentially useful resource for research libraries. Such repositories could serve as elements of a large distributed database, permitting remote storage and fast access to certain classes of documents, thus sparing smaller libraries from having to maintain their own local copies. With the appropriate software to facilitate single-copy printing and binding of these electronic documents, these sources could also serve as dissemination points for on-demand publishing, a potentially effective way to manage the distribution of older or more specialized documents for which formal publishing would not be cost-effective. With electronic scanning, it becomes possible to preserve rare and fragile documents and to make them widely available over the networks. These techniques are providing models for new, efficient forms of resource sharing, where access is instantaneous and the information delivery does not deplete the supply. These models stand in contrast to the traditional library model of local acquisition and local use and could lead potentially to the redefinition of the archival function of research libraries.

Taken together, these highly fluid network resources suggest the outline of a new information structure, not limited by the boundaries of any single institution or possessing much of a distinct structure of its own, but capable of bridging the spaces between institutions—a "virtual" library or "library without walls" some have called it. The terms may be somewhat metaphysical, but the prospect of an electronic network seamlessly and transparently linking libraries and other information sources into a single entity is not a mere fantasy. The virtual library is a reasonable extension of resource sharing goals that libraries have been pursuing for years. Pieces of such a system are already in place, and more are under construction. The pairing of interesting and unique local information sources with fast and efficient large-scale networks is a powerful combination, capable of transforming a modest desktop computer into an information-gathering device of unprecedented reach.

PROBLEMS

The network is a large and complex structure that has been built without the benefit of any master plan or blueprint and thus is constrained by no single design, but is rather the product of experiments and progressive refinements taking place simultaneously at numerous locations. This loose, organic, emergent characteristic of the network is one source of the problems that newly networked libraries are now facing: network processes do not always respect the economic, legal, political, technical, and functional boundaries within which libraries customarily operate. Much of what we thought we knew about the legal and ethical aspects of the information business will have to be relearned as library services become network services. Some of these problems are not amenable to technical solutions and will challenge the research library's ability to adapt administratively to a radically new model of librarianship. Concerns about the traditional library's ability to make the necessary changes has led pessimists to predict the demise of the library as we know it, and optimists to call for a bold reconstruction of the research library to meet the anticipated changes.

Library directors know that a research library is anything but virtual. It has walls, a roof, substantial physical holdings that must be processed, disseminated, and preserved, and a large number of users still interested mainly in printed documents and traditional services. The comments of the research library directors presented in this collection help isolate the conflicts that the new networks raise in academic library settings. Among the most vexing are the economic problems. With the costs required to perform traditional library functions already high and getting higher, and with long-term funding unstable, the prospect of extending the library's operations into a networked environment is not always very inviting to administrators involved in the budget process. Martin Runkle provides an informative account of the economic predicament of research libraries, looks at the costs of networking, and asks the reasonable question, who will pay? Government funds for network development will not be available indefinitely, and it is likely that the involvement of the private sector in the network will become more prominent as some form of privatization takes place.

Another problem raised by the current model of the national network is the lack of control. The typical academic library is founded on the principle of centralized control and organization, but the networks are, at the moment, highly decentralized and largely self-organizing. It is fortunate that groups such as the Coalition for Networked Information, ALA's Library and Information Technology Association, the Electronic Frontier Foundation, and CICNet (cosponsor of this conference), have voluntarily taken a leadership role in network research, education, and planning. But what is still notable about the Internet are the things that we do not know about it, such as who exactly is connected, what services are available at any given moment, and what constitutes legitimate network use. A few network directories exist in both electronic and printed forms, but none is comprehensive. Some loose agreements about appropriate and inappropriate network activities have been established by certain groups of network users, but there is no policy-making body and no centralized authority for monitoring network activities or controlling users and resources. Libraries taking part in such a system may well find themselves in the unaccustomed and perhaps uncomfortable role of being part of a larger institutional structure in which they do not exercise any particular authority. The decentralized library is an administrative paradox, and linking the actual library to a more abstract virtual one will probably require some retooling.

Another set of problems has to do with ease of access. There are at least two dimensions to this problem, one technical and one political. Technical expertise, experience, and specialized software are among the requirements for achieving network access, and at the moment only a small group of users possesses these qualities. The lack of standardized operating commands makes the network a hazardous environment for the inexperienced user, who must make do without comprehensive training materials or even simple documentation. Librarians dream of a seamless web of information access, but in reality the network environment is strewn with traps for the unwary. At the moment, the network is still a frontier, and untamed, but many developers believe that it will have to be civilized in order to achieve its potential. Attempts to provide better training and to achieve true interoperability are underway, but progress is slow.

The second aspect of the access question is political because it concerns network access policies. Network users are increasingly becoming a highly diverse lot, and it is not yet clear how to construct a system that can accommodate in a balanced way users ranging from kindergartners to research scientists. A particular problem is that, although the network infrastructure is supported in part with public funds, many interested potential users, including librarians eager to extend the information reach of their institutions, simply do not have a way to get in. Some fee-based Internet access points have recently become available, but in general only users at institutions that are already linked to the Internet and who have access to the necessary hardware, software, and support enjoy ready, subsidized network access. Information providers such as research labs, government agencies, and research libraries may be willing to open their doors to network users, but only the privileged few are able to take advantage of those resources. For many libraries, to learn of the network is to experience the frustration of the kid peeking through the fence at the ballpark, who can hear the cheering but cannot get close enough to enjoy the game.

The political question, it should be pointed out, has another side: not every institution is willing to leave its electronic door unlocked and may prefer to restrict access to outside users. It is a reasonable response to economic pressures. Even large computer systems are finite, and when each outside user takes up a port and consumes machine cycles, it seems appropriate for libraries to draw distinctions between their primary and secondary user communities and to offer access accordingly. At the present time, networking technology is more advanced than networking policy.

CONCLUSION

An extended process of adaptation is taking place as libraries, along with many other kinds of organizations, come to terms with their future roles in the networked communications environment that, increasingly, they all share. It is a process of considerable complexity and extended duration and is not likely to be quickly resolved. This collection of essays is presented as a contribution to that part of the process relevant to research library services, an effort that has also produced, in recent months, several national conferences, a handful of new serial publications, numerous local workshops and training sessions, and many instances of experimentation, testing, and evaluation. In keeping with the growing significance of the network communications model, many of the results of these efforts are being disseminated over the network itself, which is ultimately where the success of this process will be measured.

BRETT SUTTON
Editor

ACKNOWLEDGMENTS

The success of the conference that produced the papers in this volume was due not just to the presentations themselves, but also to the high level of discussion they generated. To conclude this introduction, we would like to acknowledge the contributions of the other invited speakers whose collective experience and insight added a valuable dimension to the discussions. These include Steve Cisler (Apple Computer, Inc.), Martin Dillon (OCLC), Carl Grant (Data Research Associates), Paul M. Hunt (Michigan State University), Ward Shaw (CARL), Bernard G. Sloan (Illinois Library Computer Systems Office), Mickie Voges (Chicago Kent School of Law), and Lou Wetherbee (Library Management Consultant).

The editors are also grateful to CICNet, the network service of the Committee on Institutional Cooperation, for its generous assistance and cosponsorship. Finally, we would like to acknowledge the indispensable assistance of Roger Clark, director of CIC, who worked as co-organizer and problem solver throughout the planning of this event.

CLIFFORD A. LYNCH

Director, Library Automation
Office of the President
University of California
Oakland, California

Networked Information: A Revolution in Progress

ABSTRACT

Progress in telecommunications and information technology has extended computer communication networks and increased network speed. With the resulting increase in networked information, questions arise as to who will control it, who will supply it, and who will have access to it. The role of the library in this electronic networked environment is changing from providing access to traditional paper-based holdings to directly acquiring material in electronic form and providing access to it. Questions arise about interlibrary cooperation, clientele, and competition for patronage. In addition, the development of the end-user workstation that will access a range of networked information resources may lead to new information markets (such as competitive intelligence) and to the potential of multimedia information access and personal scholarly publishing. The traditional role of librarians will also change. Librarians will become information specialists, skilled in the management, searching, evaluation, and organization of information. Finally, library schools must expand and refocus their roles in training these information specialists.

INTRODUCTION

The word "revolution" has been debased in recent usage. Once used to describe political upheaval and forcible rearrangement of a power structure, it is now a hackneyed advertising device: We have not only

12

the hyperbole of "revolutionary technology" but the obscenity of "revolutionary new personal hygiene products." We have become desensitized to the meaning of revolutions. In fact, there is a revolution in progress, in the old, true sense of the word: Power structures and roles are being rearranged, sometimes forcibly, though without bloodshed. Fortunes will be made and lost and power will shift; some institutions will fade and others will move to dominate.

In past revolutions, media and communications technologies have played a key role (Innes, 1972); although it seems more accurate to term the printing press, for example, an instrument of revolution rather than a revolutionary technology. The revolutions occurred long after the invention of the printing press as the presses were placed in the service of the revolutionaries.

Today's revolution is about information: about who will control it, who will supply it, and who will have access to it. Drawn into this conflict are publishers and information providers, libraries, universities, and all types of information consumers. Instruments of this revolution are drawn from the armory of information technology and computer communications networks, as well as from the blending of existing mass market consumer technologies with the computer and digital networks. These instruments are already well refined; now they will be harnessed.

Information most commonly of interest to libraries—related to scholarship and culture and typically of relatively long-term value or interest as opposed to the ephemeral, time-sensitive information that drives the daily operation of finance, business, and government—is one of the last areas to be drawn into the maelstrom of revolution. In the past two decades, the application of telecommunications and information technology has completely restructured the worlds of finance and commerce and, in a somewhat more subtle way, of government, international relations, and intelligence. Striking, suggestive parallels can be drawn between events that occurred in the spheres of finance and consumer market information and changes that are now happening in the realm of scholarly information and public knowledge.

This paper, which is based on a keynote speech given at the 28th Annual Clinic on Library Applications of Data Processing in April 1991, attempts to chart some aspects of the current revolution and the prospects for the "new order" that may result and emphasizes the fates of various types of libraries. Although a great deal of technology is surveyed superficially, the focus of the paper is not really technology but rather how technology may affect the information environment.

INSTRUMENTS OF REVOLUTION

Networks and Connectivity

Everyone is aware that networks are growing and spreading, but few realize how far and how fast. The Internet, a constellation of several thousand interconnected networks, now links between a quarter million and a million computers for interactive traffic and reaches every continent except, perhaps, Antarctica. Curiously, no one knows exactly how many computers—or individuals—are connected through the Internetwork. Furthermore, the Internet serves as a sort of core for a much larger community of users who can communicate with each other through electronic mail. This broader community of electronic mail users, which includes users of machines on **BITNET** and **USENET** and users of commercial electronic mail services such as **MCIMAIL** or CompuServe, reaches well into the millions, but again no one knows exactly how many people are really involved; and recent estimates suggest that people in over seventy nations participate. This global collection of networks is what John Quarterman (1990) calls, following the science-fiction author William Gibson (1984), "the (global) matrix." Others call it worldnet.

The Internet, and the broader global matrix, reaches many of the expected places: universities, libraries, corporations, research laboratories, and government and military sites. It is also increasingly reaching some less likely places: public libraries, elementary and high schools, and even individual homes. In certain circles, it is no longer peculiar to find ethernet cable, a router, and a class C Internet Protocol network number for someone's residence.

The massive growth of the networks was not exactly planned. The entire Internet, for example, can be understood as a research and development project that became so useful that it turned into an operational service and then grew out of control. Governance, funding, infrastructure planning, and technology development have all lagged far behind the explosive growth of connectivity; and network planners, engineers, and managers are struggling to keep up with the growth rate—dealing with problems that range from the potential exhaustion of the address space used for assigning network addresses, effective network management and problem diagnosis in very large collections of linked, autonomous networks, and security and authentication mechanisms, through the need to devise workable governance policies and funding arrangements for the Internet.

Powerful forces are at work both to extend connectivity and to increase network speeds. At the federal level in the United States, there is the movement for the National Research and Education Network

(NREN), which is based on the executive branch's proposal for a High-Performance Computing and Communications Initiative from the Office of Science and Technology Planning and the legislative bills championed by Senator Albert Gore (SB 272—signed into law Dec. 9, 1991). The NREN movement calls for massive investment in very fast networks (gigabits per second) in the 1990s. Some versions of the NREN vision also call for ubiquitous networks that will reach elementary and secondary schools and public libraries across the nation. Some state legislatures (for example, in Texas) are considering initiatives to connect the elementary and high schools on a statewide basis. In addition, strategic partnerships among state government, regional networks, industry, and both elementary and higher education are growing more extensive.

Of course, massive government and corporate computer and telecommunications networks have also been under development since the 1960s. The Internet, at least in the United States, has always been well connected to the government networks. The Advanced Research Projects Agency of the Department of Defense funded the original ARPANET network core and much of the basic research on internetworking. Part of ARPANET, split off and renamed MILNET, continues to support unclassified traffic among a large number of government and military sites. The National Aeronautics and Space Administration (NASA), the Department of Energy (DOE), and particularly the National Science Foundation (NSF) are heavily involved in the funding and operation of the current backbone networks for the Internet/NREN-to-be. Increasingly, large corporate networks are being connected to the Internet in the 1990s; today most of these belong to technology-oriented firms that exchange substantial communications with the university, research, and government institutions already on the network. But, in time, it seems likely that the enormous networks that have developed to support financial transactions, airline reservations, and other business enterprises will also be linked, at least in limited ways.

Wireless communication is suddenly becoming widely available to the general public. Car phones and portable personal telephones are everywhere and are more compact and cheaper than ever. There is a long tradition of radio-based networking arising both out of amateur ("ham") radio activities and military communications research. Both of these communities have long been part of the Internet (Lynch & Brownrigg, 1987). But now we are seeing major communications and information technology companies working on wireless network products for the commercial sector and the general public. Wireless local area networks are available, and proposals are before the Federal Communications Commission for the allocation of spectrum to support public wireless data communications. The sudden maturation of wireless networks in the 1990s is likely to produce notebook computers continually linked to the network by radio at relatively low speeds when being carried about and "docked" with larger machines connected to high-speed wire or optical fiber networks when the user is at a fixed location such as home or office. Perhaps access to the networks will become available to the general public via radio at low speeds without charge.

Existing monopolies face continual pressure. The breakup of the Bell system in the United States has encouraged the development of low-cost, high-speed trunks for long-haul communication in the United States. Today, short-haul leased lines provided by local telephone companies are often more costly than interstate lines due to politically determined rate structures set by the state public utility commissions. In Europe, there is some loosening, through privatization initiatives, of the grip of the PTT monopolies that have restricted the development of computer networking. Internationally, monopolies such as Intelsat and the treaty arrangements with foreign telephone companies, which have kept the costs of international communications links high, are increasingly questioned and threatened with competition and deregulation.

Network speeds will continue to increase rapidly. Today, the NSFNET, the primary high-speed national backbone for the Internet, is completing a transition from T1 (1.544 megabits per second [Mb/s]) to T3 (45 Mb/s); billions of packets now transit this backbone monthly. Advanced Networks and Services (ANS), the corporation formed by IBM and MCI to supply services to the NSFNET (among other things), is projecting that they will have SONET-level services (probably around 600 Mb/s) available within the next year or two. Local area networks are moving from ethernet (10 Mb/s) and token ring (16 Mb/s) to FDDI (100 Mb/s) over optical fiber. The Defense Advance Research Projects Agency (DARPA) and the NSF are funding a series of gigabits-per-second network testbeds to develop the next generation of technology. The NREN programs call for national backbones running at speeds in the low gigabits per second later in the 1990s. These backbones, as well as new local and metropolitan area network technologies, will build on experience gained from the gigabit testbeds.

After a decade of bumbling, common carriers are seriously entering the networking arena in the United States. Historically, the common carriers have merely supplied bandwidth in the form of leased lines; other organizations built networks by attaching packet switches or routers to these lines. Now the common carriers are offering potentially useful packet-switched service in the form of Switched Multi-Megabyte Data Services (SMDS), which allows transmission in the T1-T3 speed range. In addition, Integrated Services Digital Network (ISDN) technology offers two 64 kilobits-per-second (kb/s) channels to homes or offices over the existing copper cable plant. Although too little, too late for serious interorganizational or intraorganizational networking, ISDN technology could offer a considerable improvement in the ability to connect homes, small businesses, and other places to the nearest terminus of the high-speed national network. The adoption of ISDN depends on whether costs are reasonable. (And it appears they will be: The early offerings in some states are priced at about $20-$30/month for the service on use-insensitive terms within the local service area. In other states, tariff proposals have been rejected by state public utility commissions because the proposed rates were too high.)

Following ISDN is the proposed Broadband ISDN (BISDN) service, which in the early twenty-first century would offer multi-megabit data services on a commodity basis, if it actually becomes available. This technology seems to require optical fiber to the end-user premises (at the home or office); and in the United States, the development of this technology seems linked to public policy questions of whether existing cable television franchises or telephone companies will ultimately provide high-speed consumer network services. (There are several relevant public policy debates that are now receiving attention ranging from a bill in Congress for a massive program to install subscriber loop fiber optics through a revision of the rulings by Federal Judge Harold Green that would allow the RBOCs to enter information content marketplaces, thus creating a major new business justification for high-speed services.) Other countries, such as Japan, are investing heavily in the development of BISDN. The proponents of BISDN come from a rather different culture than many of the NREN's current advocates in the United States. The orientation is towards very broad-based services arising from consumer electronics and entertainment roots.

Internationally, the situation is more problematic. In many countries, high-speed leased lines are still not available within reasonable time frames and at reasonable costs, if they are available at all. Instead, the common carriers continue to promote national packet-switched networks running at relatively low speeds (64 kb/s or less), and in some cases these are costly and unreliable. It is also worth noting (Paul Peters, personal communication, April 1991) that in much of Europe flat-rate telephone service for residences does not exist, which implies that connectivity to the network from home via modem is simply unaffordable. Thus, although networks are spreading across the globe, the ubiquity of connection outside North America is still significantly constrained. The European Economic Community (EEC), for example, is still discussing how to establish a usable 2 Mb/s international network backbone linking its member countries.

The explosion of connectivity has a number of implications worth mentioning, especially under current pricing schemes, which are not usage sensitive (for end-users) and which are distance independent. The network disconnects the user from the tyranny of geography and time zones and creates electronic client-provider relationships that are distance independent as well as international communities of interest that may seldom or never meet in person but that share common concerns and communicate constantly. Information travels quickly within these communities. Connectivity will affect the spread of information about scientific discovery or political activities and, as the networks become a place to transact commerce, will create a "hot" marketplace where price may be set on a per-transaction basis.

For example, there have been proposals to conduct a marketplace in airline seats over the networks (Kuttner, 1989), which would presume the ability of the airline computers to calculate nearness to flight time, aircraft loading, historical route traffic patterns, and other factors in bidding price and which would allow customer computers to request the best bid from among all the airlines. Purchasers could choose to gamble on low prices at the last minute (due to unsold seats) or hedge against rising costs through early purchase. Some purchases might be offered preferential treatment—a direct extension of current frequent flyer programs. Such a market scheme also permits secondary market makers to appear—for example, speculators attempting to corner all airline seats between New York and Los Angeles for the Thanksgiving weekend—and then reselling these seats. Similar per-transaction models might develop for the purchase of information: "hot" authors (for example, those being awarded Nobel prizes) and "hot" topics (such as those that receive sudden national media attention or papers announcing key breakthroughs) might suddenly have their prices hiked by a publisher's computer. Of course, the meanings of old commodity-oriented terms, such as "cornering the market" and "secondary market makers," have yet to be fully defined in a hot networked information marketplace.

Such real-time markets are often unstable and notoriously difficult to manage. They are already present, to some extent, in the financial sector, where computers operated by the large brokerage houses and investment firms conduct "program trading" (a form of computer-directed multiexchange, multicommodity arbitrage) in securities and other financial instruments. According to some, this type of program training has been responsible for at least one major stock market slump (Office of Technology Assessment, 1990).

The increasing internationalization of the networks also may produce some unsettling effects. We have moved from markets governed by national laws and fixed in place and time (such as stock exchanges) to a 24-hour marketplace built from a concatenation of fixed markets across the time zones of the globe, and now these global, continuous markets are moving into purely electronic venues, divorced from any particular place or locus of regulatory control.

Import and export controls are rapidly breaking down as intangible electronic data and intellectual property move from nation to nation across the networks, and taxation of information crossing national boundaries seems impractical. Some countries, ominously, are attempting to regulate transborder data flow. For example, there are proposals that the flow of personal data be prohibited between countries that have enacted strong privacy laws and those that have not. Equally important, as the international networks develop, it becomes clear that not all countries share common cultures and legal understandings. Science-fiction writers such as Bruce Sterling (1988) have portrayed the development of offshore "data havens" in the third world where information that is regulated in first world countries can be stored and sold outside of government controls. Some nations do not seem to recognize intellectual property the same way in which most first world countries do, and perhaps the first data havens will be collections of pirated intellectual property rather than dossiers on people and organizations developed in contravention of privacy laws. This issue is of sufficient concern that it is currently under study by the United States Congress Office of Technology Assessment as an extrapolation of current problems with, for example, software piracy in Southeast Asia.

It is interesting to consider possible responses to the development of data havens as illustrations of the complexities of the new global networked environment. Other than through international diplomacy, the only way to prevent use of a data haven is to cut off access to the country that hosts these renegade databases and information services. Given the operations of the technology underpinning the Internet, however, it may be impossible to cut off access selectively to hosts in that network. And even isolating a country is very difficult. One can imagine the creation of pirate transborder microwave links to neighboring countries, shortwave packet radio links, illicit satellite uplinks, or any number of hard-to-control international connections. The battle to maintain or cut such links amounts to full-scale application of technologies developed for electronic warfare—jamming, direction finding, and low probability of intercept communications. Even the legal situation becomes murky. A user in a copyright-recognizing country displaying information from a database in a data haven may be breaking the laws of the copyright-recognizing country. But, if that user exports programs to the data haven to "mine" data stored there and only to return certain derived results, the legal status of the user's action is unclear (at least to the author).

Current controversies about cryptographic technology are an excellent illustration of the dilemmas that the global networks create. It is generally agreed that the computer communications networks are frightfully insecure and vulnerable; solving these problems requires widespread implementation of advanced cryptographic technologies such as public-key cryptosystems. Such technology (much of it simply software) is controlled in most countries by law; certainly it is restricted for export. History suggests that governments jealously guard the right to monitor communications—and most of all international communications; this practice reaches far back into the early days of the development of postal systems. Yet securing the networks requires that communications be secured with technology that may be sufficiently robust to secure it from everyone, including governments. And controlling the international proliferation of these technologies is no longer a simple matter of customs enforcement when programs can be sent from one nation to another across the networks.

Services (and Other Things) on the Networks

The purpose of the ARPANET, the now honorably retired initial network in the Internet, was to provide shared national access to expensive computers. It became clear that it also provided communication among people who were attached to the network (through electronic mail) and the ability to share software and data (through file transfer). In the early days, these applications made up the bulk of the user traffic on the Internet. The NSFNET, established in the mid-1980s, was originally intended to provide national access to high-end supercomputers that were located at a handful of NSF-funded supercomputer centers and, over time, to other high-end scientific equipment (such as specialized, massively parallel processors, telescopes, or superconducting supercolliders). Over the life of the Internet, various other specialized equipment has also been connected to the network, including elevators, soft drink vending machines, and toasters. But the service of access to specialized equipment is needed only by a small community of users. (Internet appliances, such as toasters, are still exotic and expensive, and they are not necessarily shared by large communities.)

For the majority of users today, the network provides connectivity for electronic mail, not access to information services. Yet information services are appearing, and users are starting to become aware of their existence and are beginning to try to locate and to use them. As users adapt to the idea of information services on the network and become familiar with the modest, primarily noncommercial, offerings currently available, expectations rise, and questions are asked about the information services that are not yet available through the network.

(The current situation has very important parallels with the introduction of the online catalog in libraries, which immediately led the user community to demand that the catalog be supplemented with databases providing access to the journal literature, source material, more extensive bibliographic records, and links to document delivery services.) Network-accessible information services, compared with super-computers, are of interest to huge numbers of people. They are the battlefields of the revolution, and it is in this context that the role of libraries is being called into question.

Consider the information resources available to an Internet user. There are perhaps a hundred online library catalogs publicly available (St. George, 1992), although access to the all-important journal literature abstracting and indexing (A&I) databases mounted as part of some of these online library catalogs is blocked since institutions have licensed them from database providers. There are a large number of public access file transfer archives, containing everything from out-of-copyright books in digital form through innumerable computer programs. Although these archives are treasure troves, it is enormously difficult to find anything in them.

The archives problem illustrates several interesting developments that are likely to become commonplace. Most of the archive files available—many of which are small or of relatively transient interest, such as patches to a given release of a software product—are at best described by a very brief author abstract. These abstracts do not use any type of consistent descriptive scheme or vocabulary. The contents of many of the files are programs, which do not lend themselves to automated content indexing. Thus, despite some very clever schemes such as the Archie FTP (file transfer protocol) archive index at McGill University, programs trying to provide access to the archives do not have much with which to work. The root problem is that really effective access seems to require human intellectual effort to organize and to describe the various files available, yet in most cases this effort has not been made. In fact, for many files, the value of the file does not justify the investment of such human labor. Yet the totality of the files, as a collection, is quite valuable and would be made much more so by the availability of such access tools.

There is a wide range of public access campuswide information systems (CWISs) that universities and other organizations have made available that contain information such as weather data, seminar announcements, train schedules, and song lyrics. Government data repositories are emerging, and legislation currently under consideration may increase the amount of federal government information available to the public through the Internet. There are hundreds of listservers and network discussion groups, covering everything from public access library systems to virtual reality research, molecular biology to computer communications protocols, and public policy to private pleasures (Lynch & Preston, 1990).

What is missing—but likely to appear in the next year or two— are the so-called information utilities (e.g., DIALOG, BRS, and LEXIS) and the providers of source material in electronic form (e.g., publishers). The services offered by these organizations, unlike the current public access services, will be fee based. In many cases, the transactions will be between end-users and commercial service providers. In other instances, the end-user's institution may provide subsidy as a broker/ intermediary or by establishing a site license on behalf of its user community.

The forthcoming availability of these for-profit, fee-based services presents a dilemma to the libraries in the network environment. Over the past decade, there has been talk of "disintermediation" as users become increasingly capable of accessing information directly, thereby cutting the library out of the process. In the past, disintermediation has been passive—the library has been eliminated from the process because the user has been able to access information directly, not because the user has been blocked from obtaining access to information through the library. In the past, libraries did not have a monopoly on information access; they offered a relatively efficient, inexpensive means for the user to obtain access to information (Pfaffenberger, 1990). In this sense, the impact of disintermediation during the 1980s has probably been overstated. Many users continued to obtain information through intermediaries (either librarians or professional information brokers) because they offered good, cost-effective service and because they were better than the end-user at gathering relevant information swiftly and at reasonable cost.

In the evolving network environment, however, the equation changes. Even those libraries invested in electronic information— whether as A&I databases or electronic source material—are prohibited by contract or by copyright from making this information freely available to users throughout the network. The end-user must purchase information from the information utilities or directly from the publishers. At least, the user might persuade his or her primary service provider library to license access to the information. But if the user's primary library cannot afford to license access or if the publisher will not deal with the library, then the end-user is forced to deal directly with the information provider.

If these trends continue, libraries will be displaced from their current roles by the networks and the presence of information "owners" on the networks. Libraries will continue providing access to paper-based information but will be largely blocked from using the new electronic environments for anything but the provision of access to inventories of their (increasingly less interesting) paper-based holdings. Barring major shifts in position by the information owners or major changes in the current structure of intellectual property law, the traditional role of the library will be more and more difficult.

Of course, there are opportunities for libraries to continue serving their primary clienteles in the electronic network environment. A library acquiring material in electronic form will be able to offer it to members of its institutional community. For example, a university library will be able to provide access to A&I databases or to licensed electronic source material to members of their community. But the current free sharing environment of library resources on a national level will be greatly constrained. Users will not be able to use the networks to access any library independent of geography for resources other than online catalogs. And even the institutional library serving the end-user will face direct competition from commercial services.

Particularly threatening is the possibility that the restrictions on information transfer in the evolving network environment will undermine the long and valuable tradition of interlibrary cooperation through such activities as coordinated acquisitions and interlibrary loan. The new electronic environments will continue to restrict transfer of information from one library to another, and the effect will be to cast individual libraries increasingly in isolation. They will end up competing with commercial services to support their primary clienteles rather than operating within the existing model of a national consortium of libraries attempting to provide access to information for each library's patrons.

The question of user affiliation will become terrifically important. With ubiquitous networks undermining geography, a user might theoretically seek affiliation with any library on the network—or, in fact, any set of information providers. Entrepreneurial libraries may seek "users" on a national basis; information providers will seek to limit the scope of libraries' user communities. This will be a new arena of competition among libraries and a new area for negotiation between libraries and information providers.

The issue of clientele will also take on a policy dimension, both nationally and internationally. As the electronic distribution and access infrastructure becomes established, the marginal cost of adding third world nations and public libraries to this infrastructure will be relatively small, particularly if these groups only want access to public information and older, out-of-copyright data. The question will be whether they should be given access on a marginal cost basis.

As the national networks develop, others will compete with libraries for the user's patronage. Organizations such as professional societies (who are, technically, nonprofit, but who have become large businesses and subsidize a wide spectrum of activities through their publication programs) will become extremely visible and influential as information providers. The American Chemical Society is already moving in this direction. The American Physics Society has recently issued a report from a study group exploring its role in electronic information distribution (Loken, 1990; "Task Force," 1991) and envisions the development, within the next 20 years, of a massive central physics data repository containing published journal literature, bibliographic citations, and even experimental data. The word "library" does not appear in this vision, which foresees a direct service from the physics community to the physics community, eliminating the library as an intermediary (other than, perhaps, being the organization that sends in the checks to pay for access by academic physicists). Other professional societies, usually smaller and with less secure cash flow, have already "outsourced" their publications programs to commercial scholarly publishers and thus lost control of these publications.

In counterpoint to the existing commercial and pseudo-commercial publishers, a new group of information providers will emerge: the nonprofit information providers who place a high value on public dissemination of their messages. These will include consumer advocates, religious groups of all types, government agencies, and all manner of organizations for the public good or organizations simply determined to get their message across to the public. These groups, in fact, will be eager to subsidize access to their information, in much the same way as they subsidize access today through free leaflets and mass mailings.

The Rise of the End-User Workstation

End-users are gaining more and more computing power. Within the next five years, many scholars and students will develop long-term relationships with the workstations that they are already rapidly acquiring. Today, we are at the trailing edge of time-shared computing economics; some users continue to access networked information resources via terminal emulation to an organization information system. Their organizationally provided system, in turn, helps them access other network resources. Part of the reason for this is that it still is not as easy as it should be to access the spectrum of networked information resources, and software available for end-user workstations does not help as much as it should. Another part of the reason is simply that change occurs slowly.

Within five years, I believe this situation will change radically. A user will discuss information needs with software on his or her workstation. The workstation will access a range of networked information resources (both free and for-fee service), will handle budgeting among these resources, will synthesize information from multiple sources, will learn about new resources as they become available on the networks, and will perform an active information refining function. There will be no need to involve a local, institutionally based (e.g., local library-provided) system to access commercial or free services on a national and international level. At best, files stored at the local library will be just one of many resources accessed by the workstation software, although perhaps the cost of using information there will be particularly attractive. The independence of the end-user will be the ultimate realization of disintermediation.

The technologies to support such workstation software are already in active development. These include workstation-based user agents (Buckland, 1990), Z39.50 as a common access mechanism for networked information resources (Lynch, 1990a, 1990b, 1991a, 1991b), and plans for machine-processable network information resource directories (Library of Congress, 1991), along with the necessary billing and authentication infrastructure services (Berger & Lynch, 1991).

Within the context of the rise of end-user workstations, three areas need to be addressed: competitive intelligence, multimedia, and user-driven scholarly communication. Competitive intelligence (for lack of a better phrase) is a major, largely unrecognized issue. Multimedia and end-user scholarly publishing are, in my opinion, overly promoted potential results of the workstation transition.

Competitive Intelligence

We have discussed "hot" marketplaces made possible by the networks. In a world where end-user workstations negotiate with networked information servers to access current information, some users need to know what information other users are seeking. Just as today we are beginning to see credit card companies mining their databases for salable information (for example, American Express might gain a considerable return on a finely targeted mailing list of people who spend more than $20,000 per year on airline tickets and who spend less than $1,000 per year on United Airlines), one can imagine DIALOG selling attributed searches in chemical databases by pharmaceutical corporations. There might be two rates: one where the searches are confidential, and one where the searches are available for purchase by the competitive intelligence aftermarket.

This world rapidly comes to resemble the old "spy-vs.-spy" and "spy-vs.-spy-vs.-spy" comics in *MAD Magazine*. One can imagine a pharmaceutical company commissioning the development of a computer program that deliberately searches large databases under the "resale permitted rates" and submits searches that, when analyzed by the competition, deliberately leads competitors down blind research alleys.

In a world of network-based information seeking, information and disinformation about information seeking are fungible commodities.

One can imagine as well the development of software that exploits information about who is searching what, and information that becomes more valuable as it becomes clear that more people are accessing it. Consider visions such as the Worldnet portrayed by David Brin (1990) in his recent novel *Earth*, in which users can configure personal information triggers: Show me news items in Category X that have been accessed by more than 1 percent of the network users in the past twelve hours. Such networks become complex, dynamic social and economic systems, incorporating elaborate feedback mechanisms and are subject to all manner of manipulation.

The full effects of point-of-sale (POS) tracking technology—the now ubiquitous bar code scanners in supermarkets, bookstores, record stores, and similar establishments—are just now becoming apparent. In the period during which this paper was written, two major milestones were reached. Supermarkets began to accept credit cards (at least in California) on a broad basis, permitting the collection of extraordinarily detailed data on the purchasing habits of anyone using a credit card at the supermarket. And *Billboard*, which tracks sales of recorded music, converted to POS data in the midst of considerable controversy over the fact that some very large record stores were not yet providing POS data to the firm that licenses this information from the stores, processes it, and resells it both to *Billboard* and to the major recording companies (for hundreds of thousands of dollars per company per year). The amount of very timely, very detailed data now available to track both market movements and individual purchasing habits for consumer goods will have an enormous effect on marketing and advertising as companies learn to exploit it, and a number of information brokers and refiners will profit handsomely as they help to gather and exploit these data. As the acquisition or use of information becomes more transactional, similar trends and players are likely to emerge. Circulation data may be a valuable and salable commodity for libraries (hopefully with appropriate privacy safeguards); sales data for acquisition on demand systems may become equally valuable (and will less likely contain the privacy safeguards we might like). If you use a credit card, "they" already know, or can know, for the cost of some computing cycles, a great deal about the books and recorded music you choose to acquire.

Bob Lucky's (1989) picture of executive workstations trading office gossip about who's getting raises, who's getting fired, and who's sleeping with whom on behalf of their owners may seem not only farfetched, but funny (at least the way Lucky tells it); but all it really requires is a program imbued with a bit more personality and ambition. Most of the data are already there.

Multimedia

The development potential of multimedia information as workstations proliferate has received much attention. This may in fact be chimerical: Multimedia require the author to be an orchestrator, movie director, scriptwriter, graphic artist, etc. Most multimedia today are built upon the recycling of existing musical scores, films, and images, generally in total violation of copyright laws. It seems likely that the costs of multimedia content development/acquisition will restrict development of new, "legal" multimedia to a handful of very broad-based entertainments (some with educational importance, much like today's public television programs). The average scientific communicator may be unable to develop readily legal multimedia products for distribution over the network, having neither the time, the skills, nor the licenses for components to be integrated into a multimedia work.

As an educational medium, multimedia will probably have greatest impact at the elementary to high school levels where large numbers of students study the same material, which changes very little from year to year. Here the unit cost of elaborate multimedia "textbooks" is reasonable. These costs will likely even be acceptable for introductory college courses, but it is hard to believe that it will be cost effective for advanced graduate texts and research monographs. In these areas (excepting the occasional "jewel"—a scholar's lifework, perhaps subsidized by a large grant), only modest use of sophisticated multimedia seems likely to occur in most disciplines, at least without a major revolution in authoring tools and the creation of large public domain sound, image, and video databases that can be used as source components. For routine scientific communication, text, still images, computer programs, data files, and perhaps modest amounts of audio (recorded voice) will define the scope of multimedia. The files generated by users of the NeXT multimedia mail system probably give a good sense of the level of sophistication we can expect.

A second aspect of multimedia is the problem of access to existing multimedia collections, such as film and television archives, and to new multimedia content that will be developed. Here, the prospects are equally grim. Consider a resource such as the University of California Los Angeles film and television archives. A scholar today could spend a lifetime mining a tiny part of the riches of such a collection. We do not know how to index movies or television programs for effective access, and technology will probably not provide a solution soon. Even in the more limited domain of paintings or photographs, despite the vast expenditure of resources by organizations such as the Getty Art History Information Program and the contributions of some very fine thinkers on the subject, we have only a superficial understanding of how to describe (index or catalog) a great painting, and most of the thinking to date has not been tested in a real-world environment of public access to large databases. Thus, it seems likely that effective intellectual access to multimedia resources will remain a major missing link long after these resources become accessible (in that one can view or transfer them, if one knows what one is seeking) across the network.

Personal Scholarly Publishing

Some who envision the future of networked information foresee the potential of each scholar to be a publisher. A user could store files of important research results on a workstation and advertise the availability of these files on the network, thus bypassing the existing apparatus of scholarly publishing. Scholarly information would thus be freely available. Libraries might develop new roles helping scholars to become publishers and providing catalogs of available information.

There is a basic fallacy in these visions, however, that must be addressed bluntly. For the purposes of tenure and promotion (a primary motive for scholars to publish), acceptance of a paper by a major scholarly journal is essential. Even if promotion or tenure is not at stake, professional reputation often is based on publication in the "right" journals. Transfer of copyright to the publisher—a professional society or a commercial publisher—is a basic condition of publication. There is a vicious circle here. Until personal publication on the network is viewed as having equal value as "legitimate" scholarly publication, only a few visionaries will practice it. Copyright will continue to be the major tool for restricting access to information by the commercial or quasi-commercial (professional society) publishing community, and libraries increasingly will be left out of the cycle.

Furthermore, those who do self-publish will risk obscurity for another reason: Nobody will be able to find their work. In a growing torrent of publication, increasingly elaborate A&I databases will become a primary resource for locating important literature (along with traditional methods, such as citations in other works and word of mouth). Currently, A&I databases play an important role in continuing to legitimize and affirm the status of the primary scholarly journals. It is philosophically unlikely and economically perhaps infeasible for these A&I services to cover an infinity of self-published literature, unless one postulates extensive changes in the way these services do business. For a fee, the author might submit a document to one of these services for review, and if the service favorably reviews it, then the citation to the work on the author's workstation would be published in the database. But, in such a world, the A&I service itself begins to function very like a journal with page charges. And it is only a small step, then, to having the A&I database demand rights to act as a distributor of the accepted documents.

In summary, I view the rise of the end-user workstation as the development of a very sophisticated access device to networked information resources and a potential disintermediator for libraries. As more and more access becomes electronic, new information markets (such as competitive intelligence) will develop, much as the extensive conversion of financial markets to electronic transactions (for example, the adoption of credit cards by consumers) has created (and continues to create) a myriad of new information markets since the 1960s. I do not think the workstation is a major tool for shifting the locus of control or ownership of information—although I would like to be proven wrong. Although sophisticated multimedia will be available on the networks and viewed on workstations, it will be less common and more costly than many people expect. And unsophisticated media are likely to be oversold in terms of their impact.

The Development of the Information Refiner

Almost everyone depends on information for some aspect of their personal or professional life—for example, for scholarship, business strategy, investments, or health—and, in all fields of endeavor, the information user is about to be swept away by a swelling flood of information. There are many causes: the growth in human knowledge and publication, the increasing use of electronic media, the increasing internationalization of many aspects of commerce and scholarship, the development of round-the-clock financial markets, the proliferation of sensor systems, and the development of computer-based tools that can exploit real-time or near-real-time information and take action upon it.

Services that can filter, sort, organize, and prioritize this information flood will develop in all fields in this decade. They will not, typically, create information; rather they will distill information into knowledge by collecting it from multiple sources, correlating it, and evaluating it. It seems likely that, by the turn of the century, many information seekers will deal with these new secondary services rather than with primary information suppliers. Implementations of such services will range from purely automated systems—for example, a program that scans newswires and uses a combination of keyword matching and superficial linguistic analysis to extract news items that fit a user's interest profile—to purely human-based systems perhaps as simple as weekly recommended readings sold by major authorities in research fields or abstracting and summarizing services in narrowly focused subject areas. (In the 1970s and 1980s, there was a huge growth in costly, specialized newsletters tracking developments in various fields of finance and technology; in the 1990s, these newsletters will evolve into network-based real-time services.)

In scholarly publishing, the issue will be not so much whether one can get an article published but whether a scholar can convince the various information refiners to present it to the community as worth reading. In some ways, this resembles the current situation where the scholarly journals function as "gatekeepers," but the new information refiners are likely to be quite different in character from the peer reviewers of today's scholarly journals, in ways that we do not yet fully understand. If nothing else, they are liable to be far more selective in their ratings of information and far less concerned with academic and professional courtesies.

ACCESS TO INFORMATION: THE RICH AND THE POOR

Sol Yurick (1985) authored an extremely important, but little-known meditation on the social, political, and cabalistic implications of the new electronic world, *Behold Metatron: The Recording Angel*, which should be required reading for anyone concerned with the new electronic technologies. He argues that if information becomes the new coin of the realm, then not all information will be available to everyone. In fact, information will be more tightly held and more dearly sold. We are not entering an age of universal wealth. There will still be the rich and the poor. To be sure, there will be more information than ever, with a wider range of prices than ever. Some information will be cheap and readily available—but it may not have much value. This point is often overlooked in discussions about the possible roles of libraries in the future world of electronic computer networks. Consider the three major sectors of libraries in the new universe of pervasive electronic information.

Academic (Research) Libraries

The challenge for these institutions will be to provide excellent service to their primary clientele in an environment of competition from information brokers, commercial publishers, and professional societies. They will succeed to the extent that they can subsidize access to information for which the user would otherwise have to pay and to the extent that they can add value by organizing, selecting, and refining the commercial offerings (a point discussed in the next section).

The great research libraries will face other dilemmas. Due to restrictions on licensed electronic information, they will be less able to act as the libraries of last resort standing behind public libraries, special libraries, and smaller academic libraries. For older (out-of-copyright) information, because networks will facilitate faster information transfer, smaller libraries will discard collections choosing instead, in the face of growing budgetary pressures, to rely on a few major research libraries to fill requests, thus transferring the cost burden to these few large libraries. (And these large repository libraries will increasingly recharge their real costs for servicing interlibrary loan requests.) This trend is already apparent as libraries respond to serials costs increases by canceling subscriptions and relying on interlibrary loan, but in the future, this approach will become less effective as publishers constrain transfer from one library to another through licenses to electronic information.

Furthermore, the nature of the great research library is twofold, and increasingly the two aspects are in opposition. The great research library should offer superlative service to its clientele—that is, access to information and help in locating and obtaining information. But also, the great research library houses a great collection—including things that nobody wants now but that may be critical to future scholars' understanding of the world of today. The very notion of collection is under numerous pressures in a world that is moving to electronic information. There is the sheer proliferation of material (e.g., print, electronic discussion lists, radio programs, television programs, movies, computer games, and recorded music). And there is the fact that as information rightsholders move from public law (copyright) and sale to license (contract law) for electronic information, the library does not actually own anything—it merely has a license to a set of electronic material for a fixed period of time after which it must pay more license fees.

The material of scholarship is not always economically viable. A publisher housing material on a network server for acquisition on demand may find, after a certain period of time, that the usage rate on this material is so low that it is not cost effective to keep it accessible on the network. As the cost of computing and storage drops, the crossover point will shift, but if the material is not used, eventually it will not be cost effective to keep it available for sale. The publisher is then liable to take the information electronically "out of print." In a license environment, no library will necessarily "own" a copy of this material to preserve its availability for future scholars. Mechanisms are needed to ensure that copies of such materials are maintained for future access—if not by publishers subject to the economic constraints of profitmaking corporations, then by libraries subsidized for the public good. And simply devising a code of "good behavior" for publishers on the network, which suggests that they submit materials they are taking "out-of-print" to some library-financed repository, may not be sufficient to preserve the continuity of the scholarly record.

Special Libraries

Some special libraries will behave much like narrowly focused academic research libraries; the rest will become irrelevant. In fact, it will be increasingly hard to distinguish the successful special library of the future from an academic research library in terms of services offered to the user community, except that special libraries will support a more limited set of disciplines than a university library and perhaps support them in more depth.

Special libraries may find that they have another new advantage over the larger general research libraries. Some information vendors or refiners may choose not to sell to public or large academic libraries (or to sell only at impossibly high prices) because the value of their information is in its scarcity, and they are unwilling to dilute the value over the large user communities of larger libraries. But they may be willing to market to special libraries (for example, those supporting corporate research and development efforts) because they know that the information will remain closely held. Again, the beginnings of this trend are already visible: Corporate libraries regularly acquire expensive research reports and newsletters; these are not commonly found in academic libraries. It is unclear whether this is because of the high cost of the material or because the information suppliers do not want to sell to the academic and public library sectors. Certainly, the information vendors are not marketing to these groups and are not making their materials easy to acquire—for example, they are not working much with the jobbers that service most major libraries.

Public Libraries

The future for this sector of the library community is the most perilous. Many smaller public libraries will be reduced to lending current novels and will be unable to fill other information needs for their user communities. They will have neither the funding nor the expertise to operate as intermediaries to electronic information, either as access subsidizers or refiners. In some ultimate sense, of course, public libraries are not endangered: Although scholarly information may migrate relatively quickly to electronic form, popular novels and self-help books will persist in paper form indefinitely, and thus the economics of shared acquisitions and lending for this material will continue to be viable indefinitely. The issue is the size of the constituency that the public libraries will be able to serve.

The general public will become increasingly information poor. Aside from those users who can affiliate with some academic or special library with the funding to underwrite their access to information, the general public will have to fund their own access to information or lose access altogether.

Ken Dowlin (1990) of the San Francisco Public Library uses the slogan "Ignorance kills" to emphasize the importance of public libraries as providers of information, particularly to those otherwise disenfranchised. He speaks of access to information about health, finances, community services, and educational opportunities. But, realistically, what quality of information in these areas will libraries be able to license and provide?

One often thinks of public libraries as primarily serving the adult populace, but they also fill other key roles, such as supporting primary and secondary school students and local businesses. It is in these areas that access to electronic information will be most essential to the health of commerce and education in the community, and the public library will face massive problems. Research libraries will be less able to be the provider of last resort for the public libraries due to the license restrictions already discussed. In addition, seekers of information will face a discontinuity that is already growing visible, leaving the public libraries to stand or fall on their own, increasingly meager, resources.

The currently available sources of health and medical information illustrate this discontinuity. It seems likely that some relatively low-cost "general public" databases will be developed for the mass market, perhaps at the level of current popular press articles on medical and health matters; some prototypes are already available, targeted for public library markets. But an information seeker wishing to delve even a little deeper is immediately confronted by a huge chasm: The next step is a very costly, complex, sophisticated database such as MEDLINE®, which, if the user has access to information only through a public library, is unlikely to be available unless that user purchases access personally. And, even if such access is purchased, there are the dual problems of obtaining the source material located through such a database as interlibrary loan becomes increasingly constrained by electronic information licensing and of simply understanding the citation information availability through a "specialist"-oriented database like MEDLINE. The same problem appears in many other fields. There is no longer a smooth transition from information intended for the layperson to that aimed at the specialist. And electronic information will be more complex than today's paper-based materials.

The library that flourishes in the 1990s will have to walk a tightrope across competing demands (each of which can absorb a near-infinite amount of money) to

1. continue to acquire "traditional" paper-based information;
2. acquire or provide (subsidize) access to electronic versions of the existing paper-based reference works, journal subscriptions, and similar materials;
3. acquire or provide (subsidize) access to A&I databases that provide access to the journal literature—materials held by the library as well as those available through interlibrary loan or document supply services, and existing both in paper and electronic forms;
4. acquire or provide (subsidize) access to new electronic-only forms of information: e.g., listserves, netnews, multimedia publications, numeric databases, weather information, factual databases; and
5. acquire, develop, or provide (subsidize) access to the information refinery services—evaluative, correlative, and filtering services—to control the flood of information generated by the first four demands.

A successful library in the 1990s must address all of these areas. The balance achieved will depend on the library's mission, as viewed by its management, and on the demands of its constituency. The library management must recognize that consensus is unlikely to emerge from the user community demands. User communities may fragment instead into competing factions with opposing agendas. And the most discontent of the factions, particularly if they are not advocates of expanding paper-based archives, will be fair game to competitors to the institutional library that will populate the networks.

CONCLUSION: NEW ROLES FOR LIBRARIES IN A WORLD OF NETWORKED INFORMATION

The traditional library mission has four major components:
1. to select and acquire information,
2. to house and preserve information,
3. to organize information, and
4. to provide access to information.

Compare this list of traditional functions to the pressures on the library of the 1990s enumerated above. The demand for acquisition—now generalized to encompass both traditional purchase and provision of access (via purchase-on-demand agreements or fast interlibrary loan) predominates. The archival functions are overlooked. In a sense, the archival role is sacrificed to the marginal pricing advantages of provision of access for the great research libraries. As acquisition becomes more user driven, the library's role in selecting a long-term collection is reduced. Further, more and more of the traditional library role in information organization—at least as it is understood today—is carried by copy cataloging and the purchase of A&I databases.

But there are new roles for libraries that combine elements of the four traditional missions. Libraries can play a vital role through evaluation and selection: They can choose information refiners, or they can, themselves, be information refiners.

Making the transition will require that libraries become much more comfortable in evaluating and determining the value of information. Historically, libraries' acquisitions decisions have basically been made based on information evaluation, but beyond acquisitions, they have assigned equal value to all information. There are many prototypes in progress that define librarians in new roles as information organizers, refiners, and evaluators, offering services ranging from low-cost, low-technology, but highly effective, review services, such as *Current Cites* at the University of California, Berkeley, which provides brief alerts of new and important publications in library and information science fields, through the costly, complex, sophisticated Knowledge Management process pioneered by Nina Matheson and Richard Lucier at Johns Hopkins University (Lucier, 1987, 1990). Unfortunately, for every project that involves libraries, there seem to be several that do not.

The central issue for libraries is how they can add sufficient value to guarantee their continued role in a world transfigured by information technology, ubiquitous computer networks, and massive disintermediation. Simply purchasing a role by subsidizing information access will not be enough in the long term, unless it saves a great deal of money for the institution. For institutional managers, increasingly concerned with short-term popularity, current fashions like "empowerment"—in this case, being used to justify the transfer of funds directly to the end-users and allowing them to purchase information from any supplier on the network—will have great appeal (and will attract great support from the end-user community), even though much of the library's archival function will be sacrificed in the process. Why preserve continuity of the scholarly record when the alternatives are tangibly reduced costs and empowered, happy end-users? It is possible to draw some comparisons to the restructuring of corporate America that has occurred in the past two decades? The focus on short-term profitability has, in some sense, led to an efficient corporate world, but one that promises serious weaknesses in long-term competitiveness and the development of the industrial and research base in the United States.

There are several areas in which libraries can add intellectual value. Information evaluation and filtering have already been discussed as has the creation of new information (often through partnerships with researchers) that the library can sell, broker, or otherwise control, thus placing the library in the role of primary information provider rather than simply as an information intermediary. Two other major roles are obvious. The library can organize and integrate the complex and fragmented information access environment. The beginnings of this role are apparent in the efforts of various librarians to help their communities navigate the Internet and employ the various information resources. Finally, libraries can continue to earn a role—perhaps an expanded one—as information intermediaries. It is true that more information is end-user-accessible and that the access software is becoming easier to use. At the same time, the total amount of information available is growing very rapidly, and some of it is complex and difficult to search and evaluate. Some libraries may forge effective partnerships with researchers as specialists in gathering information to support the research enterprise. If the libraries as institutions fail to do so, entrepreneurial librarians will move out of the existing library organizations in ever greater numbers to become part of research activities directly. This new breed of information specialists will combine deep area expertise with skills in information management, searching, evaluation, and organization.

Revolutions are times when the unthinkable becomes possible. One need only consider the changes that have occurred in the financial and commercial worlds since the introduction of networks and information technology to see the extent of the unthinkable changes that can, in fact, occur seemingly overnight. (To see a marvelous example of such changes, consider the trajectory of the House of Morgan from 1930 to 1989 [Chernow, 1990] from the most conservative of investment bankers to one of the most aggressive participants in the hostile takeover frenzy of the late 1980s.) Recent political events have also reacquainted us with revolutions. Who, a mere two years ago, would have predicted not only the liberation of Eastern Europe but also the breakup of the Soviet Union? The unthinkable can, in fact, happen, sometimes more swiftly than most of us want to believe. Existing institutions must rejustify their roles and value to their constituencies in the face of new alternatives for those constituencies. This is precisely the challenge that the network information revolution is creating for the institution of the library.

A POSTSCRIPT: TRAINING FUTURE
INFORMATION PROFESSIONALS

The keynote speech that was the basis of this paper was made at a conference sponsored by one of the leading schools of library and information science. Many of those present at the conference were educators and students. Thus, in closing, it seems appropriate to focus briefly on the future role of the library schools in the new world of networked information.

Although the role of libraries may be in doubt, I believe that there will be an enlarged demand for information specialists. (I do not think the term "librarian" is appropriate any more, although what are now called "library" schools may well serve as training grounds for many of these professionals.) In this sense, library schools may look forward to a promising future, if they rise to the challenge. Emerging fields such as medical informatics and large-scale scientific data management offer opportunities for library schools to expand and refocus their roles (perhaps through joint programs with other departments) in training the specialists that will be needed in the future. Following behind these immature, but now well-established disciplines, are new fields of study that as yet have no defined names but that deal with information, networks, and advanced computing technology. It is interesting that at many institutions, existing departments of computer science have not focused strongly on these new areas.

At the same time, a massive overhaul of library school curricula will be needed if these institutions are to produce graduates who can contribute to and thrive within the changed world described in this paper. Furthermore, this curriculum will have to be taught not only prospectively to people entering the field but retroactively to large numbers of established library and information professionals. This curriculum must include a comprehensive coverage of the various technologies fueling the revolution—advanced user interfaces, mass media, computer networks, and database technology. It must include study of the exploration and uses of information resources, which needs to be coupled with study of information organization and use, but from a perspective founded more on basic theory than on the mechanics of today's practices. (An excellent recent book illustrating the shift in emphasis I believe is needed is Michael Buckland's [1991] *Information and Information Systems.*) Finally, many students will also need to gain thorough knowledge of one or more applications disciplines—medicine, meteorology, finance.

This is not to say that the current, rather vocationally oriented courses need to be abolished, any more than the networked information revolution will lead to the abolition of all libraries as we know them. But the world will become more segmented, and the demand for traditional librarians will follow the diminished role and importance of libraries that remain staunchly traditional. Library schools, as institutions, need to decide whether they will look to the past or to the future. And, if the schools look to the future, they and their graduates will play a central role whether or not libraries as institutions manage to rise to the challenges of the networked information revolution. The winners of the network information revolution, be they libraries or new institutions that develop to supplant them, will require a new breed of information specialists. The library schools are the obvious training ground for these professionals.

ACKNOWLEDGMENTS

I thank Brett Sutton and Chuck Davis at the Graduate School of Library and Information Science at the University of Illinois at Urbana-Champaign for patiently waiting for this very late paper, and Cecilia Preston for reviewing and discussing innumerable drafts and for her notes on the original (impromptu) keynote address from which this paper was constructed. I also thank Michael Buckland for his very valuable comments on an earlier draft. And I thank Nancy Gusack for her editorial assistance.

REFERENCES

Berger, M. G., & Lynch, C. A. (1991). *The delivery of electronic library services: Opportunities for campus and systemwide cooperative processing* (DLA Working Paper). Oakland, CA: Division of Library Automation, University of California, Office of the President.

Brin, D. (1990). *Earth.* New York: Bantam Books.

Buckland, M. K. (1990). *Prototype for an adaptive library catalog* (U.S. Department of Education, Higher Education Act, Title II-D for Fiscal Year 1990). Berkeley, CA: School of Library and Information Studies, University of California.

Buckland, M. K. (1991). *Information and information systems.* New York: Greenwood Press.

Chernow, R. (1990). *The house of Morgan: An American banking dynasty and the rise of modern finance.* New York: Atlantic Monthly Press.

Dowlin, K. E. (1990, December). Paper presented at *Networks for Networkers II* (A preconference to the Second White House Conference on Library and Information Services). Chantilly, VA.

Gibson, W. (1984). *Neuromancer.* New York: Berkeley Publishing Group.

Innes, H. A. (1972). *Empire and communications.* Toronto: University of Toronto Press.

Kuttner, R. (1989, September 11). Computers may turn the world into one big commodities pit. *Business Week,* p. 17.

Library of Congress. (1991). *Dictionary of data elements for online information resources.* Washington, DC: Library of Congress. (Discussion Paper No. 49)

Loken, S. C. (1990, May 2). *Report of the APS Task Force on Electronic Information Systems.* Berkeley, CA: Information and Computing Division, Lawrence Berkeley Laboratory.

Lucier, R. E. (1987). OMIM: Facilitating information transfer and knowledge management in genetics. In C.-C. Chen (Ed.), *Information: The transformation of society* (Proceedings of the 50th ASIS Annual Meeting, 4-8 October 1987) (Vol. 24, pp. 259-260). Medford, NJ: Learned Information.

Lucier, R. E. (1990). Knowledge management: Refining roles in scientific communication. *EDUCOM Review, 25*(3), 21-27.

Lucky, R. W. (1989). *Silicon dreams: Information, man, and machine.* New York: St. Martin's Press.

Lynch, C. A. (1990a). Access technology for network information resources. *CAUSE/ EFFECT, 13*(2), 15-20.

Lynch, C. A. (1990b). Information retrieval as a network application. *Library Hi Tech, 8*(4), 59-74.

Lynch, C. A. (1991a). The Z39.50 information retrieval protocol: An overview and status report. *Computer Communications Review, 21*(1), 58-70.

Lynch, C. A. (1991b). The client-server model in information retrieval. In M. Dillon (Ed.), *Interfaces for information retrieval and online systems: The state of the art* (pp. 301-318). Westport, CT: Greenwood Press.

Lynch, C. A., & Brownrigg, E. B. (1987). *Packet radio networks: Architectures, protocols, technologies, and applications.* Oxford, England: Pergamon Press.

Lynch, C. A., & Preston, C. M. (1990). Internet access to information resources. In M. E. Williams (Ed.), *Annual review of information science and technology* (Vol. 25, pp. 263-312). Amsterdam: Elsevier Science.

Office of Technology Assessment. (1990). *Electronic bulls and bears: U.S. securities markets and information technology.* Washington, DC: Congress of the United States, Office of Technology Assessment.

Pfaffenberger, B. (1990). *Democratizing information: Online databases and the rise of end-user searching.* Boston, MA: G. K. Hall.

Quarterman, J. S. (1990). *The matrix: Computer networks and conferencing systems worldwide.* Bedford, MA: Digital Press.

St. George, A. (1992). *Internet-accessible library catalogs and databases.* (Available through STGEORGE@UNMB.BITNET).

Sterling, B. (1988). *Islands in the net.* New York: Arbor House.

Task force report looks at future of information services. (1991). *Bulletin of the American Physical Society, 36*(4), 1105-1107.

Yurick, S. (1985). *Behold Metatron, the recording angel.* New York: Semiotext(e).

PAUL EVAN PETERS

Director, Coalition for Networked Information
Washington, DC

Networked Information Resources and Services: Next Steps on the Road to the Distributed Digital Libraries of the Twenty-first Century*

ABSTRACT

The aim of this paper is to generate discussion about and reflection on what is meant by networked information resources and services and to provide a practical appreciation for what currently constitutes these relatively new information resources and services and how they will likely evolve as the 1990s unfold. In addition, the author hopes to convey some of the excitement that a growing number of information technologists and librarians are beginning to feel about networked information resources and services and to suggest how the efforts of those information technologists and librarians can be orchestrated for mutual benefit with the efforts of a host of other concerned and materially affected parties.

INTRODUCTION

The often-predicted and long-awaited transition from information distribution and access by exclusively print means to information distribution and access by electronic as well as print means now depends upon a variety of institutional, organizational, and marketplace

*Another version of this paper was published in CAUSE/EFFECT, Vol. 14, No. 2, Summer 1991.

"readiness factors" more than it does upon any specific technological innovation and development.

It is extremely important to place the contemporary scene in the context provided by the approximately fifty-year effort to marshal information technology to the service of scholarship and pedagogy. Doing so helps us to keep in mind what this long-term effort is really about. It is not about "electronic libraries," "virtual libraries," or even "distributed digital libraries." These popular and evocative phrases say something about the technological and service architectures that shape the efforts and aspirations of contemporary information technologists and librarians, but they say nothing about what really motivates those efforts. The mission of all of these efforts, no matter how technologically or bibliographically esoteric they may appear to be, is to improve information distribution and access by using high-performance computers and advanced networks to support research and education communication.

ADVANCED NETWORKS

So why are so many information technologists and librarians so excited about advanced networks in general and about BITNET, the National Science Foundation Network (NSFNET), the global Internet, and the proposed National Research and Education Network in particular? What's the big deal? There are three basic reasons for this excitement: simplification, connectivity, and performance.

Simplification

First of all, an advanced network provides a common framework by which to interconnect and to interoperate the great variety of highly heterogeneous departmental, institutional, regional, and other individual networks that have sprung up by one means or another over the past twenty years or so. This interconnection and interoperation results in a major technological simplification of the global networking scene and in the reduced costs and the increased values that always accompany such simplifications.

Connectivity

The second reason is that the connectivity provided by these advanced networks is expanding at a truly fantastic rate. It is becoming progressively easier and more cost effective to connect research and education communities to each other and to the growing variety of resources and services to which they contribute and on which they depend. One specific indicator of this phenomenon is provided by the growth of the NSFNET (Figure 1).

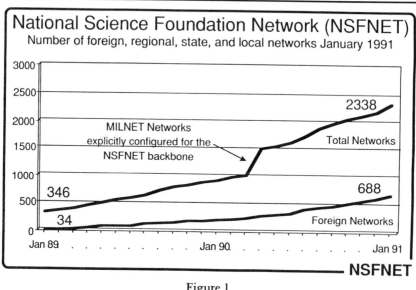

Figure 1
© Merit Network, Inc. 1991

As of January 31, 1991, 2,338 individual networks, including 688 foreign networks, can be reached through the NSFNET. In the past two years, the total number of individual networks that can be reached by this means has increased by 675 percent, while the number of foreign networks that can be reached through the network has increased by over 2,000 percent. No one knows precisely how many individual computers are interconnected by these networks or how many individual users are served by those computers, but an educated guess is 200,000 computers and 10,000,000 users. This is an impressive amount of connectivity, and it is increasing at an equally impressive rate.

Another view of the simplification and connectivity being offered by these advanced networks is provided by what they promise for library functions and interfaces. Figure 2 provides a simplified conceptualization of typical library functions and how these functions interface with a variety of external agencies and actors. For instance, the diagram shows, at six o'clock, that patrons interface with the library's reference staff and system, the library's catalog and information resources, and the library's circulation and interlibrary loan staff and systems; it also

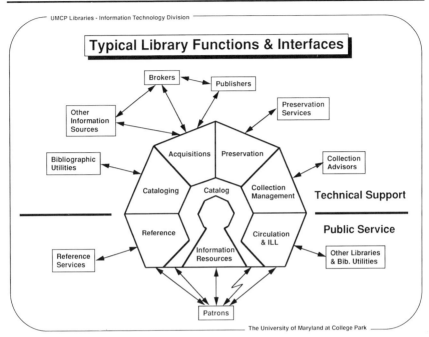

Figure 2
(Diagram courtesy of Ron Larsen, University of Maryland)

shows, at eleven o'clock, that the library's acquisitions staff and system interface with publishers, brokers, and other information resources.

Figure 3 observes that a variety of networking technologies are already being used to enhance the effectiveness and increase the efficiency of these interfaces. For instance, it shows, at between nine and ten o'clock, that private networks are being used to interface the library's cataloging staff and system with bibliographic networks such as the Research Libraries Information Network and OCLC; it also shows, at seven o'clock, that the library's reference staff and system interface with services such as DIALOG and LEXIS primarily using commercial networks.

The third and final diagram in this series, Figure 4, shows how a contemporary advanced network, shown as the large "U" that provides a setting for all the functions and a framework for all the interfaces of the library, can simplify the technological characteristics of existing interfaces while increasing the number of connections that exist among the full range of library functions and between the library functions and the full range of external agencies and actors.

Performance

Performance is the third reason why information technologists and librarians are so excited about these advanced networks. Performance levels are already mind-boggling and promise to be dumbfounding by 1995, if not sooner. Again, the NSFNET provides an object lesson (Figure 5). In January 1991, the network transported 5.87 billion packets of information that averaged approximately 350 characters each. This impressive figure becomes all the more so when one considers that it represents a 237 percent growth in traffic transported by the network in the single year that ended in January 1991, a compound growth rate for the year that averaged 20 percent per month. No one knows precisely how much traffic is transported within but not between the individual networks that are interconnected by the NSFNET, but most analysts believe that a ten-to-one ratio is a fair estimate. This estimate implies that in January 1991 alone, nearly 60 billion packets of information were transported within the networks that are interconnected by the NSFNET. This is a mind-boggling level of performance. Once again, theory predicts an exponential shape to this

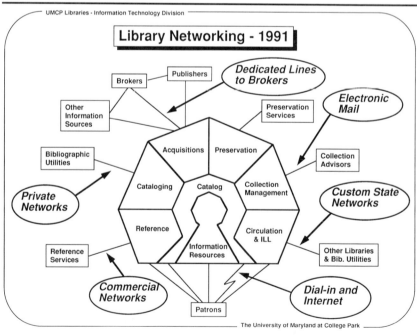

Figure 3
(Diagram courtesy of Ron Larsen, University of Maryland)

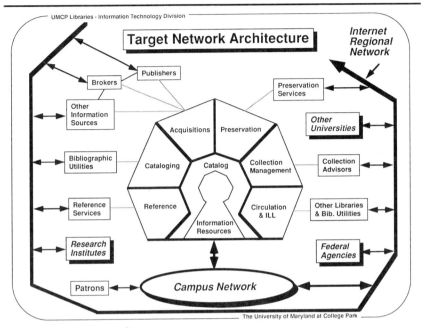

Figure 4
(Diagram courtesy of Ron Larsen, University of Maryland)

curve. Once again, we are clearly in the early stages of this growth process, or the growth process is being constrained by resources. And once again, both implications are true.

One way to try to grasp what these levels of performance mean and will mean to research and education communities is to pose the question of how many typewritten pages can be transported at a variety of illustrative performance levels. Some relatively straightforward quantitative assumptions lead to some very interesting results. For instance, if we assume that there are 200 words on a typical typewritten page, that each word has 10 letters, and that each letter requires 10 bits to encode, then we can conclude that it takes 20,000 bits to encode a typewritten page. These numbers can be used to generate Table 1.

Starting with the first line of Table 1, we see that a performance level of 2.4 kilo (thousand) bits per second (kb/s), also known as 2400 baud, enables just over a tenth of a typewritten page to be transported each second. This is the performance level of most contemporary personal computer modems and circuits when they operate at perfect efficiency. The third line of this table indicates that a performance level of 1.5 mega (million) bits per second (Mb/s) enables 75 typewritten

TABLE 1
PERFORMANCE LEVEL EXAMPLES

Performance Level	Transportation Rate
2.40 kb/s	0.12 p/s
9.60 kb/s	0.48 p/s
1.50 Mb/s	75.00 p/s
45.00 Mb/s	2,250.00 p/s
500.00 Mb/s	25,000.00 p/s
1.00 Gb/s	50,000.00 p/s

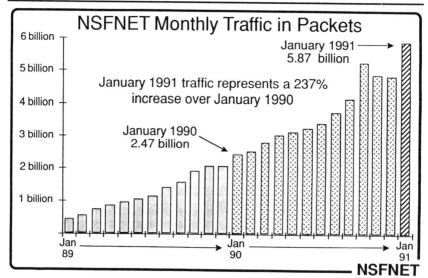

Figure 5
© Merit Network, Inc. 1991

pages to be transported each second. This is the performance level of most contemporary network controllers and circuits operating at perfect efficiency. Finally, the last line indicates that a performance level of 1 giga (billion) bits per second (Gb/s) enables 50,000 typewritten pages to be transported each second. This will be the performance level of the network controllers and circuits that will be in production use in 1995, if not sooner, when they operate at perfect efficiency.

The meaning of these performance levels can be made clearer still by considering the case of a personal library of 2,000 books. If one assumes that the typical book starts life as a 1,000-page typewritten manuscript, then it would take this personal library 40 seconds to be transported at 1 Gb/s. It would take a typical academic library of 1,000,000 books 6 hours to be transported at 1 Gb/s. It would take a relatively large research library of 5,000,000 books 1.25 days to be transported at 1 Gb/s. There are many analysts who believe that it is a much better than fifty-fifty proposition that by 1995 we will achieve production performance levels of 3 Gb/s rather than 1 Gb/s. This is a dumbfounding technological prospect; no one fully understands what it will mean for research and education communities.

ORIGIN OF ADVANCED NETWORKS
AND PERFORMANCE LEVELS

Where did these performance levels and the advanced networks that utilize them come from, and where will they come from in the future? Research and education institutions and organizations have played the most important role to date in building and operating these networks. They have played that role by making significant technological innovations as well as by making significant financial investments. Nearly every higher education institution in the United States already has a campus network or a plan by which to obtain one; by 1995, this most certainly will also be true for the overwhelming majority of research and education institutions and organizations throughout the nation.

The federal government, through the Advanced Research Projects Agency of the Department of the Army, the Department of Energy, the National Science Foundation, the National Aeronautics and Space Administration, and quite a few other federal agencies, has played the second most important role to date in building and operating these networks. However, state and local governments and related regional undertakings have recently begun to look to advanced networks to improve the educational and economic opportunities available to their citizens and residents and to enhance the effectiveness and efficiency of their many civic administrative functions such as vehicle registration, property title documentation, and the like.

Private and commercial enterprises like IBM and MCI have played the third most important role to date in building and operating these advanced networks. The role of such enterprises will become even more important during the 1990s as a result of their shift of emphasis from the analog world of switching telephone circuits to the digital world of routing datagram packets. It is very important for policy and technology planners at research and education institutions and organizations to recognize and plan the growing importance of the roles that are played by state and local governments and related regional undertakings on the one hand, and private and commercial enterprises on the other.

In this context, it is vital to recall that research and education networks have always been designed to address at least three requirements that are fundamental to research and education communities, requirements that have historically been much less important to private and commercial ones.

Horizontal Integration, Technological Diversity, and Knowledge Creation/Use

First of all, research and education networks strive for horizontal rather than vertical integration. This is to say that research and education networks are built and operated to accommodate the fact that humanists at two different institutions or organizations have more in common with each other than they do with, for example, scientists at their respective institutions or organizations. Private and commercial networks, on the other hand, are usually built to integrate the efforts of a variety of different actors in a common, vertical value or production chain.

Second, research and education networks must also account for a wider degree of technological diversity than must private and commercial networks. This mostly reflects the wide range of institutions and organizations that research and education networks must encompass, but it also manifests the high degree of innovation that characterizes research and education communities. Finally, as a general rule, research and education networks are used in a greater variety of disciplinary and interdisciplinary settings and by a more highly skilled population than are private and commercial networks. Thus the users of research and education networks are generally engaged in knowledge creation and use to a much higher degree than are the users of typical private and commercial networks.

All this will change in the 1990s as research and education networks begin to support the requirements of populations that have been typical of private and commercial networks and vice versa. This convergence is a widely predicted outcome of the conversion of industrial economies to information and services economies. As this conversion progresses, private and commercial enterprises will play an increasingly important role in building and operating advanced research and education networks. It is vital that research and education communities do not lose sight of their unique requirements during this necessary transition, and that they gauge the success of the transition by the genuine passing of the need for their vigilance in this regard.

METAPHORS FOR NETWORKING TECHNOLOGY

Before ending this discussion of advanced networks and turning attention to the information resources and services that have been and that are being enabled by these networks, the following list offers four metaphors for the future that is being created by the march of networking technology that has occupied our attention up to this point:

1. building infrastructures,
2. navigating virtual superhighways,
3. drinking from fire hoses, and
4. managing ecologies.

We are clearly building and operating an electronic infrastructure that has the potential scope and scale of the many physical infrastructures, such as road, water, and sewage systems, for which we have already mobilized the expertise and found the resources. This new electronic infrastructure will both stimulate and constrain our activities and aspirations in the same ways that these other types of infrastructures have throughout modern history.

We will conceptualize and experience this new infrastructure much as we conceptualize and experience the interstate highway system of today, the single most popular metaphor for what these advanced networks will represent to us some day. Only we will use maps, guidebooks, and other reference tools to navigate and travel in a new space that is a "virtual" rather than a "physical" presence in our lives.

Until the reality of these advanced networks measures up to the full potential of this vision, though, the experience of using them will be rather like trying to drink from a fire hose. For some time, information will gush forth from such networks at much greater rates and in much greater volumes than we will be able to capture, manipulate, or assimilate. This means that, for the foreseeable future, there will continue to be a compelling need for informational intermediaries, such as librarians and other information specialists, who will acquire, organize, store, and add value to information even though it is being distributed and accessed by electronic rather than printed means. It is even arguable that advanced networks will increase the need for such intermediaries.

It is very important for all of us, be we authors, intermediaries, or readers, to recognize that we cannot predict all, perhaps not even most, of the new things and behaviors that will emerge and occur in the new ecologies of thought and communication that these advanced networks represent. Accordingly, we need to think of ourselves as managing such ecologies as well as building and maintaining such infrastructures.

One additional metaphor will, one hopes, help to illuminate the role of librarians in this new world of networked information resources and services. At the 1991 Mid-Winter Meeting of the American Library Association last January in Chicago, Senator Albert Gore, Jr., drew an interesting parallel between contemporary librarians and navigators in the day of Christopher Columbus. Senator Gore expressed his belief that in times of revolutionary discovery, people tend to hug the shore until the knowledge of those who have made a science and an art of how to get from "here" to "there" becomes recognized and accepted. In the time of Columbus, for instance, the stature and rewards of navigators increased dramatically as a direct result of the success of the expeditions of Columbus and other explorers of the time. Analogously, the new world of research and education using advanced networks provides librarians with at least as many opportunities as it does threats. The librarians who will prosper in this new world will be those who take to heart the lesson of the navigators in the time of Columbus, a lesson that counsels that it is not the stars themselves that matter but what the stars can tell us about how we should plot our courses of action.

NETWORKED INFORMATION RESOURCES AND SERVICES

Supercomputers

Most research and education networks to date have been built and operated to provide access to computational resources and to other types of powerful and expensive scientific and technological instruments. Supercomputers represent the most important contemporary example of this type of resource. However, once the first research and education networks became operational and the uses to which they were actually being put became a subject of investigation, it was discovered that there was another resource that was at least equally, if not more, important to the users of such networks: people.

Electronic Mail, Conferences, and Journals

An analysis of the traffic being transported by the NSFNET makes the importance of people abundantly clear. As Figure 6 shows, at least 20 percent of this traffic is accounted for by electronic mail, and some very large portion of the file exchange traffic percentage results from people sending files to each other rather than from computers sending the results of computations to their users. These figures compare to the almost 20 percent of the traffic that is accounted for by interactive computational processes. New applications and extensions of electronic mail are now occurring on a self-sustaining basis. In particular, the past year has witnessed the explosion of "special interest discussion groups" such as mail reflectors and listservers and the appearance of nearly twenty refereed journals.

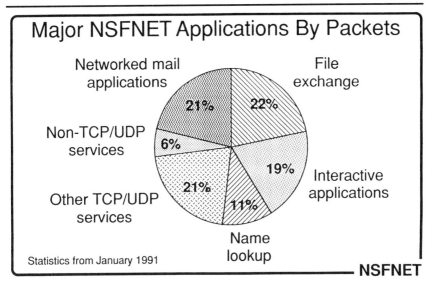

Figure 6
© Merit Network, Inc. 1991

Databases and Digital Libraries

Library catalogs and campuswide information systems represent a third category of networked information resources and services. It is this category that accounts for the lion's share of the growth and excitement in contemporary networking. Library catalogs are already far and away the most frequently found type of database on the Internet, and the databases of the Research Libraries Group and OCLC are the most frequently used "fee for service" databases on the Internet. These early efforts may not be self-sustaining—there is certainly much more to come than has arrived to date—but it is important to take note of just how quickly libraries have embraced the potential of advanced networks and how aggressively they are now seeking new ways to put these networks to work. Databases of primary research and education materials, known as "digital libraries," and of secondary materials, which provide reference information about the contents of print collections as well as the contents of digital libraries, are beginning to appear on research and education networks. The rate at which they will continue to appear promises to accelerate exponentially.

High-Volume Print Facilities

High-volume print facilities represent a relatively new fourth category of networked information resources and services. These facilities are destined to replace the generation of high-volume photocopiers that is currently in use at so many research and education institutions and organizations. They will soon offer a cost-effective alternative to the laser printers that have become such a familiar feature of academic and corporate life. These facilities will be used to print information as soon as a person finds and requests it at the institution or organization at which he or she is located. For certain types of information and users, such "on demand/on site" printing will represent a vast improvement over the current approach of printing and storing all information for all users in anticipation of demand. Insofar as most studies estimate that one-third of the cost of conventional printed research and education materials can be attributed to the inventory activities and distribution channels for those materials, this new resource holds particular promise for reducing the expense and increasing the responsiveness of acquiring such materials.

The likely impact of these high-volume printing facilities should not be discounted by the widely felt desire, at least in some quarters, for a completely electronic information distribution and access system. These facilities will allow us to experiment with a "just-in-time," in contrast to the long-established "just-in-case" information distribution and access system. They will also allow us to reconceptualize the role of paper. The role of paper in the emerging just-in-time system is as the most affordable and acceptable interface by which to access and use the information that is contained in an expanding number of electronic storehouses. This contrasts markedly to the role that paper plays in the existing just-in-case system as the exclusive means by which information is delivered, stored, and used.

These high-volume print facilities located in copy center operations may also provide an effective way to address the lack of universal access to advanced networks. Dial-up connections to information resources and services on such networks are adequate and affordable ways to look for and to find relevant information in electronic formats, but they are too slow and unreliable to be used to access such information in any volume. The ability to route such information to a high-volume print facility that is on the network and that is located at a nearby copy center operation provides the answer to the question of how to benefit from the low cost of dial-up connections to advanced networks and from the relatively large information objects that are found on such networks.

"Knowbots" and Intelligent Databases

Just over the horizon of contemporary networked information resources and services can be seen a new generation of such resources and services that apply artificial intelligence techniques in new and useful ways. Knowledge robots, or "knowbots," are algorithmic constructs engineered to wander advanced networks searching for information of interest to the human being whose interests and requirements they represent. The term *cybernautics* has recently come into use to refer to the science and practice of creating and using these network travel agents and navigational advisors. *Intelligent databases* are collections of information that are capable of knowing when and how they grow or are changed and what the significance of their growth and modification is to a variety of interested parties with whom they are in regular or even continuous communication.

LIBRARIES AND NETWORKS: PROBLEMS, PROMISES

These networked information resources and services are interesting in their own rights, but what can they do to ameliorate some of the pressing problems that face libraries and their constituencies in contemporary research and education communities? For instance, the skyrocketing costs of library materials illustrated in Figure 7 shows that serials expenditures in the 119 members of the Association of Research Libraries (ARL) increased 53 percent in the past three years while monographic expenditures increased 19 percent. The number of serials titles purchased dropped 1 percent in the same period, and the number of monographic volumes purchased dropped 16 percent. All these facts add up to the same thing: Much less information is being obtained for much more money. The larger, darker bar at the top of Figure 8 shows that nearly 40 percent of ARL members reduced their rate of acquiring new monographs by 21 percent or more in the past three years. Clearly, the attention that has been paid to what is known as the "serials pricing crisis" needs to be complemented by a heightened level of concern about what this crisis has done to the pattern of monographic acquisitions in academic and research libraries.

The size of library collections and, therefore, the amount of space that is needed to house library collections continues to expand at an exponential rate as well. One effect of the extraordinary increases in the costs of library materials has been to reduce the rate of acquisition of new materials and, therefore, to reduce the rate of growth of space requirements. But this can hardly be put forward as an acceptable way to manage a library and to address its space needs.

Another pressing concern of libraries in research and education communities is the underutilization of materials once they have been acquired. A familiar pattern emerges: Less than 60 percent of the materials in academic and research libraries ever circulate, and 80 percent

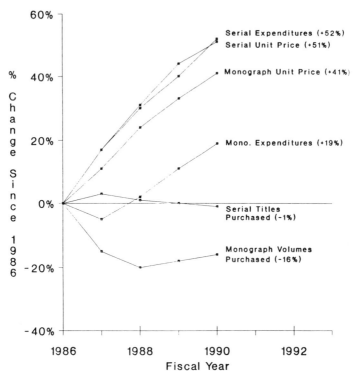

Figure 7. Monograph and serial costs in ARL Libraries, 1985-86 to 1989-90 (Stubbs, K. [1991]. Introduction. In S. M. Pritchard & E. Finer [Comps.], *ARL Statistics 1989-90* [p. 6]. Washington, DC: Association of Research Libraries)

of the materials that do circulate do so relatively soon after they have been acquired. Too many analysts have been all too quick to explain this phenomenon by decrying the declining quality of the literature record. But information cannot be used if it cannot be found, and better access mechanisms increase levels of use. This has been repeatedly affirmed by collection use studies performed both before and after the advent of online library information systems.

Thus the use of networked information resources and services promises to reduce the costs of acquiring library materials, to stabilize the rate of growth of the space required to house library materials, and to increase the rate of use of library materials. It is not yet clear that these specific promises will in fact be realized, but a great deal of contemporary effort is motivated by the hope that they will.

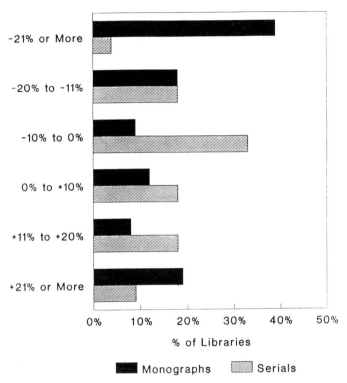

Figure 8. Percent change in monographs and serials purchased, 1986-90 (Stubbs, K. [1991]. Introduction. In S. M. Pritchard & E. Finer [Comps.], *ARL Statistics 1989-90* [p. 8]. Washington, DC: Association of Research Libraries)

Cost/Benefit of Networked versus Print Resources and Services

Two things are very clear in the extremely complicated and somewhat theoretical area of the "cost/benefit" performance of networked information resources and services as compared with their print equivalents. First, the transition from card (paper) form catalogs to online ones may have something to tell us about the transition that we may or may not now be making from paper-form publications to electronic ones. In the author's experience, card catalogs collapsed and became unworkable under the pressure of the information explosion. Something quite similar is happening now with printed primary research and education materials: the existing system is collapsing and becoming unworkable. No matter how difficult it is to imagine, the transition from an exclusively print to a progressively more electronic information distribution and access system may well be something about which we have very little choice, and it is certainly something about which our constituencies may have no choice at all.

Second, research and education communities, and particularly their libraries, are beginning to shift toward a "make" posture and away from a "buy" one as the business strategy by which they gain access to the information resources and services that they need. In addition to the cry to "take back the rights" that is heard in contemporary forums devoted to the serials pricing crisis, a new call is voiced to "take back the means of production." This new interest in self-publishing, both personal and institutional and in partnership undertakings that build new networked information resources and services in not-for-profit and barter settings, is well worth watching and experimenting with.

Networked information resources and services also promise to improve access to brittle books that have been preserved on microfilm and then digitally scanned, and to enable library services to be available around the clock and from any point on the campus network. These resources and services allow faculty, students, information technologists, and librarians to work together to effectively manage the information and knowledge that is essential to the integrity and success of all research and education communities.

Networked Resources and Information Systems Design

Networked information resources and services also force us to rethink the design assumptions of most of the current generation of local library information systems. Most such systems assume that they are providing service to a smart user using a dumb terminal right around the corner from a large computer that contains descriptions of information owned by the library. The problem is that in today's world, we are all dealing with "dumb" (i.e., inexperienced) users who are using personal computers and workstations located almost anywhere to access computers of all sizes to obtain information that is sometimes neither owned nor licensed by the same institution or organization that owns or licenses the computer. Designers and vendors of such systems are well aware of how completely their systems need to be rethought in terms of a "networked information" rather than a "housed information" architecture. The buyers and funders of such systems now need to recognize this fact and to account for it in their strategic plans and, even more important, in their depreciation schedules.

Redesigning local library information systems is only one of the things that we need to do to get ready to benefit from networked information resources and services. In general, research and education institutions and organizations must focus on improving their readiness in four key areas: campus networks, the automated library, skilled and equipped end-users, and hospitable culture. It is tautological to say that campus networks have to become ubiquitous, affordable, and responsive for the promise of networked information resources and services to be realized. It is equally important to have a vital, evolving library technology program and a skilled and equipped group of end-users. But these three readiness factors, no matter how necessary, are not sufficient. Efforts directed at these factors need to be planned and executed in a cultural setting that is hospitable to their purposes and problems. Promotion and tenure practices, for instance, need to recognize and reward excellence in authoring networked information as well as recognizing and rewarding excellence in authoring printed information. Accreditation and statistical practices and criteria need to rate libraries on how well they deliver information as well as on how well they buy and maintain information. And information technologists and librarians need to work together to construct a "single information system image" for the faculty, students, administrators, and other stakeholders who depend so much on their vision, talent, and energy.

It is also extremely important to recognize that contemporary efforts devoted to advanced networks provide the opportunity to merge two quite different and equally powerful research and education networking traditions. During the 1970s and 1980s, librarians were funding and building the Research Libraries Group and OCLC, arguably the only integrated, nationwide applications of networking that the research and education community have ever successfully made. During the same period, information technologists were funding and building the ARPANET, BITNET, the NSFNET, and the global Internet, among other advanced networks. What we are about right now is the leveraging of each tradition to the benefit of the other and to the benefit of the constituencies that are shared by librarians and information technologists.

THE INFORMATION MARKETPLACE

The readiness of the information marketplace must also be improved in at least five key areas—pricing, payment, protection, regulation, and experimentation. The marketplace does not currently know how to price networked information, and even if it did, we would not know how to pay for that information in all the ways and by all the schemes we need. The marketplace has not come to agreement on ways and means for protecting networked information from unauthorized modification as well as from misuse and misappropriation. The regulatory framework by which "conduit" is differentiated from "content" is extremely fragile, having resulted from a series of ad hoc rather than deliberate decisions. The result is that some lines of business are not allowed for some enterprises, and some activities are judged to produce "unrelated business income" for some research and education institutions and organizations. Finally, experimentation with new networked information resources and services is too costly and risky and the results are too anecdotal for all parties involved. We simply must devise a much more satisfactory system of research, development, and dissemination than the one we have at present.

Coalition for Networked Information

The Coalition for Networked Information is particularly devoted to identifying and addressing such institutional and marketplace readiness factors. Its mission is to promote the creation of and access to information resources in networked environments in order to enrich scholarship and to enhance intellectual productivity. Founded in March 1990 as a joint activity of ARL, CAUSE, and EDUCOM, it has grown like wildfire to a membership of just over 135 separate institutions and organizations. The real story of the Coalition's membership, though, is told by the variety of information, service, and technology providers that have joined numerous research and educational institutions and quite a few collaborating professional and scholarly societies in a common program of work devoted to a shared vision of how the nature of information management must change through the end of the twentieth century and into the beginning of the twenty-first.

SOME FUNDAMENTAL QUESTIONS

Four questions are fundamental to realizing the full promise of networked information resources and services, questions that all concerned parties, not just information technologists and librarians, can relate to and help to answer.

First, the technical question: What benefits can be realistically achieved? We have to find a way to spend less time on wishful thinking and more time on improving the performance of the systems and technologies that we already have. We must figure out ways to get new value out of these existing assets. We must also be ready, willing, and able to change the way we have been doing things to leverage these existing assets to get more things done faster and without a loss of quality. But the major thrust of the technical question is the pressing need to improve our ability to hold technology accountable to providing real benefits to real people.

Second, the political question: Who will experience these benefits when using what resources? This question has an economic as well as a political component but, especially in the United States, the political component is much more important. We must figure out ways to become more concerned than we have been to date about how access to the benefits of networked information resources and services is obtained. We also must become better at remembering that diverse user populations enrich and strengthen the design and performance of technological systems.

A third question calls attention to the role of institutions like libraries in consolidating the gains of technological advance. It is the institutional question: How will these benefits be secured and routinized as soon as possible? We must figure out ways to refit institutional and organizational facilities, to reallocate institutional and organizational budgets, and to re-skill relevant institutional and organizational professionals if we are to succeed at embedding networked information resources and services into the milieu of research and education communities.

Finally, we must assure ourselves that what we do contributes to improving the basic conditions of human existence and that we can explore that concern by asking the human question: Why will these benefits contribute to the quality of life and the inspiration of intellect? Without applying this test to our activities and aspirations, we can never know whether we are working on the things that can make the greatest difference in the course of human affairs.

CONCLUSION

Our facility with the technical question will determine whether networked information resources and services will become as useful as we hope or will, instead, become sandboxes in which technophiliacs play with their new and quite expensive toys. Our facility with the political question will determine whether these resources and services will become opportunities available to all who seek to learn and think or will, instead, become battlefields on which conflicts about ends and means reflect differences in opportunities. Our facility with the institutional question will determine whether networked information resources and services will become familiar and trusted features of the libraries of research and education communities or will, instead, become the products of new marketplaces in which financial means play a disproportionately influential role. Finally, our facility with the human question will determine whether networked information resources and services will become esoteric tools used by limited populations for narrow purposes or will, instead, become "fields of dreams" for which the guiding principle is, "If we build them, the users will come."

SUSAN K. MARTIN

University Librarian
Georgetown University
Washington, DC

Defining "It":
NREN's Opportunities for Librarians

ABSTRACT

Various aspects of the National Research and Education Network (NREN) are discussed. Legislation currently under consideration is characterized by a focus on the research community to the exclusion of other potential user communities and is also characterized by a low level of federal funding. Librarians have already played a role in changing the focus of the proposed network and need to continue this effort. Other issues discussed include defining when the Internet evolves into the NREN, who will have access to the network, what will be accessible on the network, and who will pay for access to the network. Finally, the role of the librarian in a leadership capacity in the implementation of the network is discussed.

INTRODUCTION

In recent months, the opportunities stimulated by Senator Albert Gore's (D.-Tenn.) vision of an information highway for the nation have caused many people to have visions of free access to all information for all people, in this country and in others. In March 1991, the Coalition for Networked Information met, followed immediately by the EDUCOM National NET'91. Coming from those two meetings was a clear sense that although progress is being made, no one really knows what "it" is; that is, what the National Research and Education Network (NREN) really is or will be. Given this situation, we may not even know when it comes into existence. We think we know the general direction that the information society is going, and because we are a profession concerned with the access to and management of information, this phenomenon is going to be critically important to us. But we can only begin to guess what the landscape will be like, who the stakeholders will be, and suggest in what ways we might contribute to and participate in the national network.

What are some of the issues at hand that we need to recognize? There are a host of rather difficult questions to address; some will have to be addressed by the library community alone, whereas others should be addressed in concert with those communities (academic, administrative, computing) that have already chosen to ally themselves with us in the pursuit of this vision.

LEGISLATION

Legislation, which librarians thought well in hand, continues to be a problem. At this writing, Senator Gore's bill, apparently noncontroversial and ready to go last year, is not safely tucked away with the sufficient number of votes. He has reintroduced his bill, and there is a companion House bill, but there is also a bill being put forward by the Senate Energy Committee because of its lack of satisfaction with the Gore bill. In addition, the whole education community is working with the Senate Labor and Education Committee to attempt to bring to the fore some information policy issues that remain unaddressed by the Gore bill.

When Gore's bill was reintroduced in February 1991, the Congress was challenged by the administration to pass it within one hundred days, which would have been some time in May 1991. The good news is that there is bipartisan support for the bill and no serious disagreement between the White House and Congress, although White House Science Advisor Bromley apparently believes that this can be an administration effort alone with no assistance required from Congress. This relatively minor point alone seems insufficient reason to derail the legislation.

The bad news is that some, including voices from the library world, are questioning the advisability of a piece of legislation that envisions a network focused primarily on the research community. The Senate Energy Committee has its own agenda. It is unhappy with the governance structure suggested by the bill and believes that the provisions of the bill will not adequately support the national security, access, and governance concerns of the Department of Energy. Governance is only loosely addressed in the Gore legislation. As it turns out, the library community shares the concerns of the Senate Energy Committee and for a very understandable reason: each group believes that as the statute is currently designed, its own vested interests will not be seen as critical in the administration and operation of the network.

For example, the management structure as envisioned by the administration is a Federal Networking Council composed of the National Science Foundation (NSF), the National Aeronautics and Space Administration, the Department of Energy, the Department of Defense, the Environmental Protection Agency, the Office of Management and Budget, the Office of Science and Technology Policy, and a few other federal agencies perceived by the Senate Science and Technology Committee as operating programs requiring network support. This council is to be subdivided into working groups and supplemented by an advisory body that has on it representatives from the Library of Congress, the National Library of Medicine, and the National Agricultural Library, among other federal agencies. However, this council, with its policy-making power and its advisory council, is not included in any legislation. Which governance structure will prevail? And how will the nonfederal sector participate?

The Senate Energy Committee may suggest various options for governance, among them a national networking council, a nonprofit corporation analogous to the Corporation for Public Broadcasting, the Federal Networking Council, or the FCCSET (the Federal Computer Council for Science, Energy, and Technology). Any one of these, they posit, could oversee "it"—and let me remind you here that it is still unclear what "it" is. Is the network something that stands alone, is clearly identifiable, and can be governed by a single body? Only a few months ago, IBM, MCI, and Merit joined together to form a not-for-profit organization, ANS, that would implement and operate the NREN. They are not alone in looking toward the increasing desire to network as a source of profit.

The network exists already, is in use, and there is a large and growing customer base already accustomed to having access to certain facilities through the network at a cost that is generally absorbed by institutional budgets. With the NREN governance structure as proposed, there is the advantage of presumed continuing federal support and the promise of wider access to a publicly held program, but these are assumptions and presumptions. The legislation still leaves too many important decisions up to a small group with relatively narrow interests, and it also represents a low level of federal dollar investment.

The dominance of federal agencies in the legislation, and therefore in the way we tend to perceive the structure today, is not comfortable to many. Remember that the name of the legislation is the High-Performance Computing Act of 1991; it is not the National Research and Education Network Act. The NREN is only one part of the legislation, which is based on a long-standing relationship between government agencies and university science and technology research. From the perspective of the federal government and its agencies, the purpose of the network is to better enable communication between federal employees and federal government contractor scientists. The fact that the rest of the university community has acquired access to this network is not recognized by either the administration or Congress, and this will remain the case until librarians begin to demand characteristics, performance, and costs that are unforeseen by the science-oriented agencies and the drafters of the various pieces of legislation. The existing network structure is governed in large part by the NSF and includes regional networks, which are important to the current operations but which are totally ignored in the legislation. These regional networks are closer to the users of the network, are more diverse, and are not totally federally funded, but they represent the investment of state funds and institutional dollars. The proposed governance places all the voice in Washington, which is not necessarily where it should be.

As the American public learns of the network, there will be a sufficient outcry that the governance structure and concomitant issues will have to change to meet the outstanding needs. With libraries' legislative support and contacts, librarians are in an eminently suitable position to talk to their representatives in Congress about the desirability of creating a network that can serve more than just the scientists of this nation.

THE E IN NREN

The E in NREN stands for Education. It was not always there; in fact, librarians played a prominent role in causing the E to appear in NREN. Before early 1989, it was just the National Research Network—designed to support scientists in their contractual work with federal agencies.

The E was put into NREN, but is it more than just a sop? We need to better determine our role in the development and implementation of this network. We have to tell Congress and the public why the E is in NREN, and what it means for the network and for the population of this country. We have not done that very well yet but seem to have sat back on our laurels, having done the alphabetically difficult task of inserting the E. We have to follow up by convincing Congress, federal agencies, and our colleagues that this is an essential capability for schools and libraries in enhancing the productivity and education level of the nation. It is almost as though the creators of the concept allowed us to have our way by inserting the E, but nothing else has really changed. And that is unacceptable to me; it should also be unacceptable to you.

What is the library community's role, then? One obvious one is to continue to lobby Congress, directly and through our professional associations, to urge them to accept this conceptual change and to regard the network as the beginning of a nationwide communication system that will have as much impact as the telephone system, if not more. The benefits of the system need to be described more precisely and should balance public good and private gain. I once talked with a senator who was totally enraptured by the concept of a ten-year-old boy in a rural area of his state being able to communicate with and learn French from someone elsewhere in the country or even in France; we need to develop realistic visions of how the network will be used by the public, and why it will be good for the country.

Also concerned are the publishers and other for-profit organizations, with copyright, intellectual property, and the profit-making issues as motivating factors. This is particularly important because Congress and the White House have made the assumption that NREN will ultimately move to the private sector. If this network is going to be a vitally important tool for the nation, who will pay for it? Just as some are making an analogy with a supposedly free highway system, there is an analogy with the telephone system that we have constructed in this country. Assume that the Gore bill passes and that funds are appropriated. The funds will be used for research, for the overhead needed to coordinate the network, for a "directory" of resources on the network, and for special grant-assisted projects. *Government funding will not support the routine operation of the network.*

What can the average person, or the average library, assume that he (or it) will gain from the passage of the bill and the appropriation of funds? Equipment? No—that is a local cost, unless someone successfully writes a grant proposal for a project that addresses some activity described by the bill. Communications costs or cabling? Unlikely. First of all, most of the country is already networked; the funding in the bill will go toward the research necessary to develop higher speed networks and not toward the implementation and operation of these networks.

Most important for librarians will be the cost of accessing information on the network. Later in this paper, I will address in more detail what resources are likely to be on the network. For now, let me suggest that the appropriate model for libraries is a mixed economic model. With the exception of "free" information such as library catalogs, conferences, and electronic mail, much of the benefit of the network will result from accessing databases held by the private sector. Right now, libraries pay differently for online databases, generally linked to the nature of the original publisher of the database. In turn, libraries make a determination about how the costs will be passed on: in some institutions, full cost recovery, both direct and indirect, is implemented; in others, the library subsidizes all online searching; most of us are somewhere in between. With the NREN, I suggest that database publishers will not make their information available through the network until they can be assured of compensation for access to those data. As opposed to being a "free good," NREN access may merely facilitate access to increasingly higher cost information.

WHAT IS "IT?"

The Internet exists. It is a network of networks and institutions evolved from the NSFNET and governed by a group of peers. Most of us in academic environments have access to BITNET, a network of academic computing facilities; this has evolved in many instances into access to the Internet as well. It seems quite clear that NREN represents the next stage of evolution of this nationwide and worldwide network. There are, however, some amazing ambiguities and a very fuzzy border between today's Internet and tomorrow's NREN. It may not matter very much what the distinction is between the two, but the fact is that people perceive a difference, and, as they say, perception is all-important.

When does NREN become NREN? Some of the possibilities include the following:

1. when the Gore bill passes;
2. when legislation is not only passed, but funds are appropriated;
3. when a gigabit network exists;
4. when NSF or OSTP (or some other federal agency) says so;
5. when a governance structure is in place.

Even the experts admit to being confused about this question. Some are beginning to say that it does not matter because the NREN will be just a small portion of an evolving national network that will come into existence over the next few years. Peter Likins (1991), president of Lehigh, said at National NET'91 that he sees NREN as an academic precursor for a *broader private telecommunications infrastructure for this country.*

Let us frame the question differently: when the Gore bill passes and is funded, will it make any perceptible difference for libraries? I suggest that it will make a difference, but that we will not notice it because the bill, and NREN, are part of the evolving network scene that we are already engaged in. Instead of focusing on NREN, we need to decide what we, as a community, want to provide our users from the nationwide network that may or may not be NREN.

ACCESS

Instead of trying to decide, then, when Internet will become NREN, let us look at the kinds of capabilities we, as research and academic librarians, want for ourselves and our users. In a word, we want *access*. In the best of all possible worlds, for librarians, we would have free, unregulated, and unlimited access to as much information as is reasonably possible. And we want equitable and relatively low-cost access. Equitable means that whoever seeks information should be able to get whatever information is available on the same terms as any other person seeking that information. This is putting into practice Jefferson's ideal of a democratic society. There should be no distinction between information seekers on the basis of income, education, or other place in society. That is a very general statement and is subject to all kinds of protest and caveats, but as a whole, this is the ideal world. Given that, librarians should start out with that operating assumption and only give up the ideal when forced to by necessity or by compromise. Clearly this means expanding our interests beyond the academic community. Low cost is an ambiguous term, but again it attempts to convey a principle and a reality: the principle is that if people do not need to pay, they should not have to, and the reality is that information, like everything else, costs money.

Librarians want access to the network by the entire education community, from kindergarten to the postgraduate and research community. This vision evokes the national network concept. Some would say "Kindergarten? Are you serious?" But there is a community of interest lobbying for access to the network on behalf of all schools and teachers in the United States. After all, if we are to have a productive citizenry, should not children have access to a national network at the earliest possible age? A major question is the matter of cost of access for thousands of teachers and millions of schoolchildren. Is it possible that our society will gradually be willing to use tax dollars to pay for access to the network in the public schools or tuition dollars in the private schools? Institutions of higher education, and their libraries, need to perceive that access to the NREN by the K-12 population will have a distinct impact on the resources required for higher education in the future, and librarians should be taking an active interest in the broadened reach of the network.

Librarians want availability of the system for independent, unaffiliated users, whether for research, education, or business purposes.

Right now, if you are not associated with an institution of higher education that is an Internet node, it is complicated and sometimes expensive to get an account on the network. This question resembles that of providing academic library access to unaffiliated scholars; our society is not set up well to deal with people as individuals rather than people as members of institutions. It is certainly easier to deal with institutions, but we must ultimately come around to coping with the question of how to give that community access to the electronic information resources at our disposal, just as we have already determined that public libraries are the way to give them access to print information. Public libraries may continue to be the appropriate mechanism in a networked world as well.

We want to seriously explore the possibility of linking to the NREN governance structure the existing nationwide networks that support the exchange and delivery of information. That means the current regional networks for NSFNET and Internet, but it also means OCLC, RLG, and some of the other information and library-oriented services that have been in place for one or two decades, have established user bases, and provide significant information services to the country.

Turning now to specifics, what will NREN give access to? Considering that the NREN is an evolution of the Internet, we can hazard some reasonable guesses. Electronic mail and computer conferencing are two obvious and early suggestions. These have already changed our lives; the Faxon Institute conference held in April was preceded and followed by a two-month-long computer conference, made available to the speakers and attendees at the conference to share ideas before and after the meeting. The electronic mail capacity of the system is saving time that used to be spent trying to reach people who were never available. Now one just leaves a message in a mailbox, and the addressees respond whenever they can—perhaps at midnight or on weekends—but they do respond. We have not worked out all the bugs; there is no central directory in which one can look up user ID's; it is still difficult to send messages to Europe; and I continue to have trouble with CompuServe—but all in all, electronic mail is a useful facility that changes the very nature of our communication processes.

Another resource already on the Internet is library online catalogs. Librarians rapidly embraced the Internet's capabilities. This seemed like a good idea at the time. It is unclear at this point whether it really is sensible to make individual library catalogs universally available. Let us look at some conditions under which access to online catalogs is useful, and others under which it may be at best misleading. For the faculty member at an institution that has a catalog accessible through

Internet but not in any other dial-up mode, the availability of the catalog online is clearly useful. These catalogs may also be useful *if* you know what you are looking for or *if* you know the strengths of the libraries represented in the Internet. On the other hand, if a researcher is attempting to find a specific item and does not care where it is held, having two hundred individual library catalogs online through one Internet will be only frustrating. In one of the recent online conferences, there was a discussion of the use of online catalogs on the Internet. I could characterize these communications as inconclusive; some are delighted at the availability of all this bibliographic information and are busy teaching students and faculty how to use it, whereas others are certain that a hundred catalogs blooming on the Internet will not be helpful to the researcher.

The availability of researchers' files on the network is of considerable interest. In reality, though, many research-oriented files are, if not copyrighted, at least considered proprietary by their creators. We still do not know very much about the way in which scholars exchange information and under what conditions they are willing to do so. More and more, the products of research efforts are closely held and, less frequently than in the past, shared with the community of scholars—especially if that community's size cannot be predicted because anyone can have access to the network. It will be necessary for some research to be done to identify conditions under which information can be shared versus those conditions under which files are to be held privately. It is clearly within the scope of the library profession's research interest to address this topic in a manner that will have an impact on the world of scholarly communication. Who else can better examine and describe the ways in which people access and use information?

Among the easier conditions to examine, ironically, are the published databases; that is, the databases produced by the private sector that have royalties associated with their use and that we are already using through brokers such as DIALOG and BRS. As the information publishers and brokers become comfortable with the concept of a nationwide network, and as they are able to confirm that they can charge per access, print, or download, they will make their databases available throughout the NREN. All the appropriate business structures are in place; licensing fees have been developed, site licenses exist, and the private sector has begun to recognize that access to its information online could be a better deal than they had originally anticipated. Libraries will have to cope with the question of how to charge. Will they subsidize access to these databases? Or when someone wants to access a commercial database, will they have to use special passwords or account numbers so that they can be billed, either at cost or at a subsidized rate?

Noncommercial databases will also be relatively easy to handle. Here, one presumes that data are being made available to the world at large; the database creator neither worries that his ideas will be stolen nor that he will not receive recompense for the use of the data. The issues here are ones of ease of access, including standardization of searching, location of the database in a directory, and related issues that, considering the alternatives, will not be serious impediments.

NETWORK ACCESS COSTS

Some librarians are adamant that if they cannot offer a service without charge, they should not offer it at all. I disagree with this approach for two reasons: (a) it is unrealistic given the way our society interprets the interaction between the public and private sectors, and (b) there is plenty of leeway to allow libraries or their parent institutions to make distinct decisions about subsidizing access to information.

The costs of accessing the network are not at all clear, but my suspicion is that access will not be cheap. We have a wonderful tendency to ignore discussion of costs when we talk about the future network. The Coalition for Networked Information has seven working groups; none of them is treating cost as an issue, at least at this point, although most of the topics addressed by the working groups have direct cost implications.

Thus far, we know that public funds will not pay for the support of the network and that the intention is to move the operation of the network into the private sector. We also know that the NREN will require wiring, equipment, software, and training, among other things, all of which cost money. Where do librarians think the funds will come from to support this? The direct answer to this question is, I believe, that we are *not* thinking about this issue at all yet, but we *should* be.

Libraries, when confronted with whatever set of costs will be associated with NREN, will have to make decisions. Should the library continue to be on the network? If so, who is going to pay for access? Will the costs be passed along to the end-user, or will the library subsidize access? What about access by the user directly from his or her personal computer at home? Will the cost structure be different for home access, causing people to turn more toward the library for access? I cannot answer these questions, and I think librarians as a community can only speculate about them at this time. But we should be lining up our arguments, just as I said earlier that we should assume the most ideal situation and fight for compromises from that extreme rather than beginning with an already negotiated stance.

Let me qualify what I have just said because this position, taken to extremes, can be counterproductive. We need, as a profession, to stand up for the best interest of our users. However, if we are perceived as being unrealistic and unwilling to deal and negotiate, we will be ignored. That happened to a part of the library community last year during the discussion of the Paperwork Reduction Act; I strongly suggest that we do not want to have a similar occurrence in the future.

WHAT NEEDS TO BE DONE

We, as librarians, need to raise our voices. We are being heard, and our representatives in Congress are doing an excellent job; however, I do not think that most of the Senate or the House realize that librarians may have an interest in the NREN. They need to get letters. One very important thing that can be done, both before and after the bill is passed, is for librarians to write their Congressmen, urging passage of the bill, indicating the intense depth of interest in it by the library and education communities, and urging appropriation of funds.

Librarians also need to educate the research community. These are the people who invented BITNET, who have been using networks for file transfers and electronic mail for years. They need to become aware that their communication and computing tool is about to be used by a very different community within the academic setting and by a population outside academia. We need to tell them what is happening and why we are urging wide access to the system, and we need to gain their support.

We have created our own opportunity to raise the awareness of the wider library community, elected officials, and library users. The White House Conference on Library and Information Services will be held July 9-13, 1991. Many state conferences have sent forward recommendations that the government support the NREN and particularly the educational role of NREN. The delegates to the White House Conference have the opportunity of ensuring that NREN emerges as one of the major recommendations for support and as a target of opportunity for our society in the coming decade.

LEADERSHIP

Can librarians be leaders in the implementation of the NREN? It is not farfetched to assume that librarians, and particularly academic librarians, can and should push themselves forward to participate as equals with researchers and computer scientists. First, we already have the Coalition for Networked Information. Librarians are nominally an equal partner within the three participating groups, two of which are computer professionals. In fact the majority of the attendance at meetings, and the active participation, comes from the library sector. This must continue. Second, we must remember that it is all well and good to link computers by laying fiber and using communications technologies, but people must perceive a *need* to send information back and forth, and it must be more than electronic mail to justify the great expense that is foreseen by the NREN. What happens on university campuses? The engineers and scientists implement a campuswide network without a good idea of what will flow over the lines. One of the first resources widely used is the library catalog and other library-related information databases.

So librarians *are* already *among* the leaders, and we can lead in some very specific areas. In part, this issue is a problem of the public stereotype of librarians. Nonlibrarians are surprised to find that the library community not only knows about computers and information technology but has also been on the cutting edge of the development of these technological applications. This is a wonderful opportunity to address the stereotype and to show others that librarians do more than check out books.

Most important, however, are the issues of service and information delivery. Librarians understand how to organize information and how people use, seek, and acquire information. They also understand the kinds of problems and issues they run into in the process. If the library had invented BITNET, do you suppose that there would be no directory of user names or of available resources? The documentation for use of the system would be far more adequate for the purpose. (I say this with apologies because BITNET is a wonderful tool, but it does have its drawbacks.) Librarians must step forward to assume the role of service provider and information disseminator for networked information, just as we have been able to do for information in print. In individual cases, on individual campuses, this may well represent a strong partnership between the library and the computer center. In a public environment, it is likely to be the library alone. Nonetheless, people will need help in order to find what they need, and the library profession is the appropriate group to help.

Librarians will be leaders, and we will be able to play a significant role in the way that information is brought to all levels of education and need throughout this country. Self-confidence, and assuredness that we are capable of having this kind of impact, is the foundation of all that is needed.

REFERENCE

Likins, P. (1991, March). Information highways: Who pays? Paper presented at the EDUCOM National NET'91 Conference. Washington, DC.

JAMES E. RUSH

Executive Director
PALINET
Philadelphia, Pennsylvania

Keeping the Window of Opportunity
Open for the Private Sector

ABSTRACT

If libraries are to grow in the coming years, they must redefine the services offered, the clientele served, and the mechanisms for financing operations. Through existing regional telecommunication networks and the proposed National Research and Education Network (NREN), libraries can de-emphasize physical collections and become virtual libraries, providing global access to information—not only to their traditional clientele but to business and industry as well. By serving the private sector, libraries can contribute to the economic growth of society; however, by charging for these information services, they may do so on a profitable basis. PALINET is developing a program that will enable its members to deliver fee-based services to business and industry; this program could serve as a model for services that would be available on a national network.

INTRODUCTION

Much has been said and written about the advantages that will accrue to libraries as telecommunication networks become ever more pervasive and as access to these communication facilities becomes easier. However, the assumption that underlies such talk and writing seems to be that the clientele of individual libraries will remain largely

74

unchanged. This assumption has been invalid for a long time and cannot be allowed to remain unchallenged in the networking environment of today and tomorrow.

The importance of timely and accurate information to economic development and growth cannot be overstated (Koenig, 1990; McAdams, Vietorisz, Dougan, & Lombardi, 1988). Access to information cannot, therefore, be restricted to our traditional clientele. Nor can we simply continue to provide access to traditional sources of information.

Although some public libraries have built support for business and industry, few academic libraries have done so. Dougherty (1991) has written recently that research libraries need to be more "user-responsive." Size, as he points out, is not the central concern of library users; access to information is. But Dougherty clearly views the clientele of research libraries as students and faculty. Libraries in general and research libraries in particular have a responsibility to society that is larger than this traditional definition of client implies. It is essential that libraries forge partnerships with business and industry that will provide greater benefits to our society as a whole than is possible under our present mode of operation.

Networks, data in machine-readable form, and emphasis on access make a redefinition of our role economically feasible. Libraries of all types must have as their primary objective the delivery of information to people in all walks of life. In the words of Frederick Kilgour (1979), "when and where they need it" (p. 202).

Therefore, libraries face a critical choice, one that we must make before it is made for us. We must either redefine the services we offer, the clientele we purport to serve, and the mechanisms for financing operations if we are to grow and prosper in the coming years; or we can choose to live out our declining years doing business as usual.

For several years, telecommunication networks and computer-based processing have enabled libraries, especially large libraries, to choose between these two alternatives. Unfortunately, most have so far chosen the second alternative. The implications of this choice are obvious.

Libraries must either seize the opportunity to which existing and planned telecommunication networks give rise, and therefore play a significant and major role in this country's economic development and global competitiveness, or live out their declining years in a caretaker capacity. Libraries of all types, and academic libraries in particular, both large and small, have an immensely important role to play in economic development and improvement of the general quality of life in this country, but that role remains to be pursued with vigor.

Every segment of society needs information and will have it whether or not libraries are willing to provide it when and where needed. Let us seize the opportunity to redefine our organizations and our profession before that window of opportunity is forever closed to us.

After the presentation of some background information and a look at the options available to business and industry for accessing information, a program we are planning at PALINET (Pennsylvania Area Library Network) to help forge alliances between our member libraries and business and industry in our region is outlined.

BACKGROUND

The idea of the virtual library, part of the title of this clinic, is not new. What the term implies is that libraries need not—indeed, should not—be architectural monuments or warehouses of artifacts, but sources of information. Data communication networks make the virtual library possible, as many have observed (Molholt, 1988; Battin, 1985). Few libraries have, however, worked hard to become virtual libraries, although there are some that are clearly moving in that direction, e.g., Pikes Peak Library District, CARL (Colorado Alliance of Research Libraries), Carnegie-Mellon University, Lehigh University, and Dartmouth College. At the same time, few automated library systems are adequately designed to support the virtual library, although the CARL, PALS (Project for Automated Library System [Unisys Corp.]), and Data Research Associates Inc. (DRA) ATLAS systems are at least partial exceptions.

One item of concern about the condition of libraries is that it has taken so long for the idea of the virtual library to be spoken of openly, much less acted upon. The lack of vision this indicates does not bode well for the future of libraries.

In a speech before a meeting of the Library Association of the City University of New York early in 1975, the author said,

> Libraries today are isolated, independent entities, paid for by many but used by few. Libraries are, in the minds of many people, equated with the buildings that house them. In contrast, what I envision is a single universal library, the union catalog of which may be found in every home. The technology to put a universal catalog in every home is available now. (Rush, 1976)

To be sure, my vision was less than adequate, for it is not the catalog that is important, but the data to which the catalog points, and it is not only homes, but offices as well, from which access to the universal library may be gained.

Six years later, the author was also the keynote speaker at an ASIS regional conference on "The National Library Network: Perspectives for the 1980's" (Rush, 1981). That speech argued that a national network would develop from the grass roots upward, rather than be developed from on "high." A seven-level national network of networks was proposed, a concept that grew out of work the author was doing for

INCOLSA (Indiana Cooperative Library Services Authority) in 1980 and 1981. This conceptualization embodied distributed processing and distributed databases. The OCLC system, which the author helped to design and implement, reflected this concept, albeit within narrow geographical confines—the system is all in one building.

This idea of a network of networks was further refined and expanded upon in a paper prepared for the Library of Congress Network Advisory Committee at its April 23, 1983, meeting (Rush, 1983). The network envisioned there grew to eight levels, numbered 0-7, wherein level 0 was an international (global) network, and level 1 was a national network. The lowest level, level 7, consisted of individual workstations, terminals, and small local area networks. In all of this, the emphasis was on the processing capabilities of nodes in the network rather than on the communication facilities linking processing nodes.

Of course, that vision was not novel and was short of the mark in several ways, but it clearly represented a model that gradually is being implemented. It is gratifying that some ten to fifteen years later, the idea of the virtual or universal library is being taken seriously. However, this idea is far from being universally accepted within the profession.

Today, there are many networks that fit at various levels within the model first presented in 1981. What is now being considered is a new network at level 1, the National Research and Education Network (NREN), ultimately to supplant, or at least impose some order on, the plethora of networks now operating at this level (Catlett, 1989).

SCOPE OF THE NREN

A network designed to link other networks on a nationwide basis and to provide the gateways to other nation's networks is now being pursued (Getz, 1989). This network, NREN, is a very important facility for nationwide, if not global, information access and delivery, but this technological marvel must not become the tail that wags the dog. It is not the telecommunication facility per se that is important, but the data that flow over it.

Inasmuch as the NREN will cost a great deal of money to implement, it is appropriate, as Likins (1991) pointed out in a speech before the EDUCOM National NET'91 Conference, to ask, "Who benefits?" Every one, that is, society at large, should benefit. Research and education are not limited to the formalized rituals practiced in our academic institutions; neither are they restricted to one's years of formal education nor just to science and technology. Therefore, the scope of the NREN, which is already being expanded through the influence of the Coalition for Networked Information, needs to be broadened further to be as all-encompassing as possible. Likins (1991) has observed that

> in the federal budget, NREN is viewed as the academic precursor to the future development of a broader, privately operated national information infrastructure, an infrastructure which is essential to the evolution of a competitive US capability in the global economy. Unless consumers, businesses, hospitals, schools, libraries and governments are all linked together in a way that permits convenient and cost-effective exchange of all kinds of information, we will be unable to compete in a global economy that values knowledge and its application above all else. (p. 4)

If the window of opportunity is opening for research libraries to create the universal library, then we must keep the window open for the private sector—"companies large and small that drive our economy" (Likins, 1991, p. 5).

ACCESS TO DATA BY BUSINESS AND INDUSTRY

Many large corporations are able to afford their own in-house information centers. Even so, much of the information used by clients of these centers comes from outside sources, including other libraries.

However, most private enterprise is carried out by small- to medium-sized corporations, and these organizations rarely can afford to operate an in-house information service. It is the small corporation that is often the most innovative and thus most in need of timely and accurate information. But it is the small corporation that can least afford to invest staff time and other resources to obtain the needed information on its own.

It is for this reason that libraries must develop capabilities for providing information to business and industry. However, such capabilities should not be provided free of charge. Libraries must develop sound policies and practices for charging for information services, particularly when they support business and industry—the private sector.

PALINET MODEL FOR REGIONAL NETWORKING

In order to assist the members of PALINET in delivering meaningful services to business and industry within our service area, PALINET is planning a three-phase development program intended to provide a broad spectrum of information services to our members that they can deliver to their clientele, with emphasis on business and industry. The three phases and the nature of the services each is expected to provide are outlined in the following pages. The reader should bear in mind that we are just at the conceptual stage of planning, and that PALINET's Board of Trustees has only authorized work at this stage. Whether or not PALINET actually implements some or all of the plan is a decision that will be made by the board when the time is right.

It should be emphasized that the services we are planning are intended to be delivered wholesale to our members who will, in turn, retail them to their clientele. PALINET has no intention of competing with our own members for delivery of information services within our service area. Rather, we want to facilitate delivery of services to business and industry through our members and through other libraries that may become members of PALINET. The implications of this approach will become more evident later in this paper, but it should be obvious that larger libraries could implement a similar program unilaterally.

Phase 1: Network Interfaces/Electronic Mail

The first phase of our planned development is quite simple and straightforward. This phase involves establishment of an interface between the PREPnet (Pennsylvania Research and Economic Partnership network) and PALINET's electronic mail system, CALL (Computer Access Linking Libraries). This will provide all PREPnet users easy, quick access to a capable electronic mail service, and obviate the need for PREPnet to implement such a service itself. The interface will also permit PALINET members to communicate not only with other organizations in Pennsylvania but also with libraries and other organizations throughout the world through PREPnet's gateway into the Internet (Quarterman, 1990). We expect to support the free flow of electronic mail between other services and CALL, so that CALL users may send mail to people on the Internet and vice versa. This service will emphasize a problem in internetwork access that needs to be resolved soon: addressing (Ohio State, 1990). Just as ordinary voice telephony employs a standardized addressing scheme worldwide, so must our data communication networks. We cannot continue with the chaotic addressing situation that presently exists.

Phase 1 establishes the communication links that will be needed by Phases 2 and 3. It is a relatively low-cost first step toward delivery of information to business and industry.

Phase 2: Economic Development Information Service

The second phase of our planned development is more ambitious. In this phase, a larger computer system would be installed, and the

CALL system would be migrated to this new platform, also interfaced to PREPnet. In addition to electronic mail, Phase 2 would bring into operation an information service offering a variety of databases that are beneficial to economic development but that are typically difficult to gain access to, at least while the data are current. Such databases include

- census data;
- industry production data;
- real estate data (including such things as listings of commercial and residential real estate, title information, sales data, and the like);
- directories;
- budgets of public agencies;
- tax information;
- legislation pending and enacted;
- compensation of all public employees;
- standards and regulations;
- capital investment sources;
- grant sources for innovation;
- organizations that assist start-up companies;
- community information;
- databases created and maintained by the library;

and much more. In addition, gateways to existing reference services, such as EasyNet, OCLC's EPIC Service, and DIALOG, would be provided.

The most difficult aspect of this development phase will be establishment of a reliable supply of data from a wide variety of sources and establishment of working arrangements with existing reference services.

In addition to database supply, Phase 2 would provide PALINET member libraries the opportunity to retail specialized data to business and industry. Access would be provided through workstations in the library, offices, and homes. Authorization to access the data would be managed by the library so that the service would appear as a library service rather than as a PALINET service. Moreover, the library would be relieved of the need to collect money, perform billing and accounting functions, and do other administrative chores.

Although the library might choose to subsidize the service (a practice the author discourages), payment by the user would be made via deposit account, bank card, or credit card, all managed by PALINET. On all sales, the difference between the wholesale and retail prices would be credited to the PALINET member account, and such revenue would then be available to the library for any purpose of the library.

Phase 2 would establish expanded processing capacity, increased communication capacity, an economic development information service, and a mechanism for handling payment for services.

Phase 3: Library Support Services

Once Phase 2 is completed, it becomes a relatively simple matter to add support for basic library operations such as acquisitions, serials control, circulation control, and public catalog access. Any novelty in Phase 3 lies in the fact that such support would be delivered to the library by PALINET and charged for on a transaction basis. This is a concept the author proposed at OCLC in 1977 but that was never implemented. Nevertheless, variations on the concept have been implemented in several places, including Connecticut, Indiana, and Illinois. It is just the service bureau model with transaction charging rather than time and materials charging.

The importance of this approach to providing automation support for library operations is that it enables even very small libraries to take advantage of quite robust systems at a cost commensurate with their needs and ability to pay. Moreover, it obviates the need for capital investment, system management, software and hardware upgrades, system replacement, and other work that is associated with owning and operating a computer system. In addition, it insures that all participants are networked.

CONCLUSION

If libraries are to grow and prosper in the coming years, they must change. One of these changes must be in the definition of the clientele the library purports to serve, with particular emphasis on business and industry.

Libraries must cease to build physical collections and become virtual libraries by supporting and providing, via regional and national networks, access to information in electronic form. Libraries must also provide access to information to any and all who want or need the information and have the means (either direct or indirect) to pay.

Libraries have the opportunity to serve business and industry on a profitable basis and should pursue this opportunity before it is seized by other organizations.

Regional networks such as PALINET have a role to play in enabling libraries to achieve these objectives. The PALINET program outlined here could also be undertaken by larger libraries on an individual basis, but the services they provide must be available throughout the national network.

ACKNOWLEDGMENT

Thanks to Berry Richards, Director of Libraries at Lehigh University, for her generous help in preparing this paper. Of course she bears no responsibility for the remarks contained herein, nor should one infer that she necessarily agrees with them.

REFERENCES

Battin, P. (1985). The electronic library—A vision for the future. In H. Liebaers, W. J. Haas, & W. E. Biervliet (Eds.), *New information technologies and libraries* (Proceedings of the Advanced Research Workshop on the Impact of New Information Technologies on Library Management, Resources, and Cooperation in Europe and North America, November 1984) (pp. 201-218). Dordrecht, The Netherlands: D. Reidel.

Catlett, C. (1989). The NSFNET: Beginnings of a national research Internet. *Academic Computing, 3*(5), 18-21.

Dougherty, R. M. (1991). Needed: User-responsive research libraries. *Library Journal, 116*(1), 59-62.

Getz, M. (1989). National Research and Education Network. *Bottom Line, 3*(4), 32-35.

Kilgour, F. G. (1979). Sharing resources in computerized systems. In H. D. L. Vervliet (Ed.), *Resource sharing of libraries in developing countries* (Proceedings of the 1977 IFLA/UNESCO pre-session seminar for librarians from developing countries, 30 August-4 September 1977) (pp. 202-207). Munich: K. G. Saur.

Koenig, M. E. D. (1990). Information services and downstream productivity. In M. E. Williams (Ed.), *Annual review of information science and technology* (Vol. 26, pp. 55-86). Amsterdam: Elsevier Science.

Likins, P. (1991, March). Information highways: Who pays? Paper presented at the EDUCOM National NET'91 Conference. Washington, DC.

McAdams, A. K.; Vietorisz, T.; Dougan, W. L.; & Lombardi, J. T. (1988). Economic benefits and public support of a national education and research network. *EDUCOM Bulletin, 23*(2/3), 63-71.

Molholt, P. (1988). Libraries and the new technologies: Courting the Cheshire cat. *Library Journal, 113*(19), 37-41.

Ohio State offers campus e-mail that fills in the address blanks. (1990). *Manage IT, 1*(4), 1.

PALINET News. (1988, November). 43, 6.

Quarterman, J. S. (1990). *The matrix: Computer networks and conferencing systems worldwide.* Bedford, MA: Digital Press.

Rush, J. E. (1976, April). *The effect of technological innovation on libraries and librarianship.* Paper presented before the Library Association of the City University of New York Meeting.

Rush, J. E. (1981, September). *The national library network: A practical perspective.* Paper presented to the ASIS Regional Conference on the National Library Network: Perspectives for the 1980s. Ann Arbor, MI.

Rush, J. E. (1983, April). *Computer-based library networks: What are they? How are they developing?* Paper presented at the meeting of the Library of Congress Network Advisory Committee. Washington, DC.

CHARLES E. CATLETT

Manager, Networking Development
National Center for Supercomputing Applications (NCSA)
University of Illinois at Urbana-Champaign

and

JEFFREY A. TERSTRIEP

Project Lead, Networking Development
National Center for Supercomputing Applications (NCSA)
University of Illinois at Urbana-Champaign

The Use and Effect of Multimedia Digital Libraries in a National Network

ABSTRACT

The Internet has supported information archives for some time. These archives have traditionally allowed users to retrieve text and image data as well as software to their own computers for examination. As the Internet grows in scale and in performance and services, more sophisticated information archives and access modes are possible. This paper reviews the growth of the Internet with its current information archive services and proposes methods for providing interactive access to multimedia data. Various information types and their access modes are discussed in terms of their role in defining advanced digital library and network services. A prototype digital library system and user interface developed at the National Center for Supercomputing Applications is examined.

BACKGROUND: THE GROWTH OF THE INTERNET

The term *internet* means a network of networks. Our national network today is composed of a number of national backbone networks

84

(e.g., NSFNET, ESNet), mid-level (regional, consortium) networks, and campus networks. "The Internet" is a network of networks that includes our national network as well as other connected networks in many countries throughout the world. The common thread among all Internet components is that they operate based on the same network protocols and share a common addressing scheme, message forwarding (or "routing") schemes, etc.

In looking at the growth of the Internet, it is helpful to look closely at a major component of the Internet, the NSFNET. In 1986, the National Science Foundation (NSF) established the NSFNET to interconnect six supercomputer centers at 56 kilobits per second (kb/s). At each backbone node, mid-level networks were established. The NSFNET architecture consists of a *backbone* network, *mid-level* networks to extend the backbone connectivity to institutions, and *campus* networks to extend the mid-level connectivity to individual local area networks (LANs). By 1988, these mid-level networks were providing backbone access to over 500 individual sites. In late 1988, the backbone was expanded to thirteen nodes, and the links were upgraded to 1.5 megabits per second (Mb/s). By the fall of 1990, the network had grown to over 2,000 sites, and the backbone was again upgraded to sixteen nodes interconnected at 45 Mb/s.

During the past several years, a number of international links have been established as well, including extensive connectivity to Europe and the Pacific Rim. Campus networks have matured, providing access to many more individual computers so that now the Internet connects over 300,000 individual computers. Figure 1 shows the rapid growth of the Internet. Hosts on the network are shown from the original, centralized host registration at the Network Information Center (NIC) as well as the current decentralized registration system called the Domain Name System (DNS). "NSFNET Backbone Traffic" refers to the number of data packets that are transported across the NSFNET backbone network monthly. Note in particular the growth in foreign (non-U.S.) networks connected, the number of individual hosts, and the growth in the amount of data being passed over the NSFNET backbone (Smarr & Catlett, in press).

It is not at all clear where or when this growth will level out. A large emphasis is being seen now in connecting K-12 institutions to the network, and the various mid-level networks are beginning to concentrate on marketing the network to a number of sectors including industry and education.

"DIGITAL LIBRARIES" ON THE INTERNET TODAY

A number of academic library catalog search systems are accessible from the Internet today. CICNet interconnects Big Ten universities and several others. The library catalog search facilities of the libraries of most of these universities are accessible from the network. These services deliver only information about where data exist but do not provide access to the actual data.

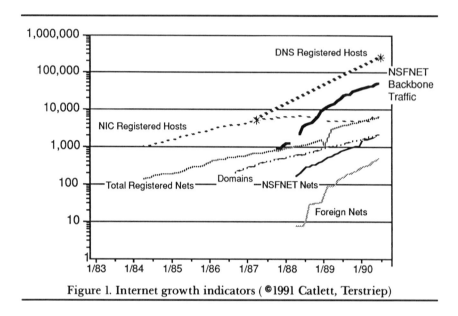

Figure 1. Internet growth indicators (©1991 Catlett, Terstriep)

Internet services that provide access to information are currently limited to archives reachable via file transfer and bulletin boards. An advantage to these services is that they are globally accessible, and the fact that they are heavily used in spite of their shortcomings indicates the demand for these services, which provide access to text, software, and images. Images and software as well as large text files are generally compressed, and the user must decompress them (once they have been retrieved) before using them. This makes the file opaque from the user's point of view. The user must also have access to the facilities required to run any of the available software.

The archives that allow file transfer have a number of limitations. First, there are no universal indexing or naming conventions; therefore, it is difficult to locate items. Second, an item must be retrieved in full before it can be examined beyond reading the file name. Given that file names do not provide any significant indication of the contents of the item, users do not have a viable means to screen items before transferring them over the network to examine them. Third, there are few directories telling users where to find these archives or what is contained in any of them. These archives, then, are useful if one knows what one needs, where it is, and how it is stored.

Bulletin boards are slightly better in that the information is organized in categories. There are several hundred categories generally accessible. However, these categories consist mainly of computer science and popular culture topics. Within a category, there is no index of contents beyond the title (subject) of the entry, the author, and the date. There are a number of software packages available to read these bulletin boards. Many are difficult to use, requiring extensive experience even for simple filtering of information such as searching for entries with a particular subject. Some of the recent access packages that run on Apple Macintoshes, however, provide a fairly straightforward user interface.

Most computer centers operate a storage archive for their users. These large private collections are not generally accessible for general users. Those that provide general access use anonymous file transfer protocol (ftp) as described above. These archives cannot be ignored, if for no other reason than their size and growth rate. A typical major computing center's storage archive can grow at between 50 and 200 Gbytes per month.

Large-scale projects that are underway and require more sophisticated digital access include the Human Genome Project, the Hubble Space Telescope, the Earth Observing System (EOS), and the BIMA (Berkeley-Illinois-Maryland Array) radio astronomy imaging consortium. In the case of the Hubble Space Telescope and the EOS, it is estimated that up to 1 terabyte per day will be collected.

CONTENTS OF A MULTIMEDIA DIGITAL LIBRARY

The scientific multimedia digital library will contain a variety of information types. Table 1a shows the approximate size of various types of data. This table includes individual items, such as images or journal articles, and their average sizes. From the size, one can calculate the network throughput required to retrieve them in a fixed amount of time. Sequences of data such as image sequences, audio, etc., are shown in Table 1b along with the approximate network throughput required to transmit them.

In addition to standard types of data such as those shown in Tables 1a and 1b, the scientific multimedia digital library also contains data sets generated by applications such as numerical models. Direct access to data sets would allow scientists to verify the conclusions of their colleagues by examining the data firsthand. Also, for such applications as global climate models that require hundreds of hours of supercomputer time to run, a number of users will want to "mine" or explore the data.

TABLE 1A

VARIOUS ITEMS (AND THEIR SIZES)
FOUND IN A MULTIMEDIA DIGITAL LIBRARY*

Item	Size Calculation	Size in Bits
Journal articles, papers, etc. (avg. 5 pages)		
Plain text	5 kbyte/pg. × 5 pg. avg.	25 kbytes
Formatted text	10% overhead to text = 5.5 kbyte/pg. × 5 pg. avg.	28 kbytes
Scanned page images	300 dpi × 7.5 in. × 10 in. = 1 Mbyte/pg. × 5 pg. avg.	5 Mbytes
Single images		
Color NTSC	512 × 512 × 8 bits	.26 Mbytes
G4 FAX	1.7 k × 2.2 kbits	.5 Mbytes
Gray-scale	2 k × 2 k × 8 bits	4 Mbytes
Color	2 k × 2 k × 24 bits	12 Mbytes

*Calculations on the average size of each item are shown as well as the size.

TABLE 1B

SEQUENCES OF DATA AND APPROXIMATE NETWORK
THROUGHPUT TO TRANSMIT

Sequences	Heading	Required Throughput
Audio		
Low fidelity	Sampling rate	.064 Mb/s
High fidelity	Sampling rate	.64 Mb/s
High-definition TV*		
Production quality	Minimal compression, 30 frames/second	1-2 Gb/s
Post-production quality	Modest compression	200 Mb/s
Distribution quality	Compression with information loss	20 Mb/s
NTSC quality	Compression with information and visual loss	5 Mb/s
VCR quality	Compression with significant information, visual loss	1.5 Mb/s

*HDTV compression rates are from Glenn Reitmeier, Director, High-Definition Imaging and Computing Laboratory, David Sarnoff Research Center.

The scientist will want to examine the data in a number of ways, including extracting portions of information at the byte level. It is critical that the data be stored in such a way that their format and contents can be later ascertained. There are a number of data file formats that are generally used in the computation science community. These formats incorporate a standard header describing the contents of the data file as well as access software for reading, writing, and interpreting the headers. Self-describing data formats might also contain references to data analysis software or perhaps copies of appropriate access and analysis subroutine object code and source code.

The multimedia digital library might also store programs that generate the data rather than the actual data. For example, periodic complete state information (checkpoints) of a long global climate model might be more convenient to examine than the multiple terabytes of data that the model could generate. In this case, the user will generate the data "on-the-fly" by starting up the model at some point in the model's cycle.

Images and sequences of images will be stored in the multimedia digital library as shown in Tables 1a and 1b. Note that the output from a data generator application could also be a sequence of images such as this. Scientists require at least distribution quality imagery for serious examination, although lower quality may suffice for cursory examination or observation of large-scale phenomena (e.g., weather patterns in a climate model).

THE SCIENTIFIC DATA MANAGEMENT FACILITY

A Prototype Multimedia Digital Library

The National Center for Supercomputing Applications (NCSA) is developing multimedia digital library services for a number of projects, including the implementation of a central archive for the BIMA project, storing scores of data sets and images collected by the Hat Creek millimeter array radio telescope. The intent of much of this work is to explore the provision of interactive access to the types of objects that a scientist would find useful in a multimedia digital library.

A prototype has been designed based on several fundamental components of a multimedia digital library aimed at providing access to information used by computational scientists. The data involve multiple formats and media types. The data will be distributed, will in many cases be pre-existing, and thus will have a set format and storage type and must be accessed in that way.

Two major components make up the digital library: directory services and data access. The digital library can be accessed using a variety of applications, including, for example, user interfaces with browsing and examining capabilities and data analysis packages to examine data.

An indexing system or directory service is needed to provide a catalog of location and, preferably, format/type information for the distributed data archives. This function is essentially a database with information about the location of data items, the type of data, and the format of the data. This component is a database.

A mechanism for locating data is needed to access the digital library; this will query the directory database. Mechanisms for browsing data and for examining data are necessary. The mechanisms will differ for the various data formats and media types. In the case of data generators (programs) in the digital library, index entries include information about where the data generator will be executed.

Figure 2 illustrates the functional components of the digital library as implemented in a prototype that was demonstrated during March 1991 at National NET'91 in Washington, DC. This includes the user interface with browsing and examination applications as well as the directory and data archive components. Figure 2 also includes multiple archives with multiple item types, including data generators and the use of data analysis filters.

The scientific digital library prototype has several indexes and several data archives, and some indexes reference multiple archives. The user interface sends queries to one or more indexes. The queries result in lists of relevant items sent to the user, each with one-line description, author, creation date, data type, and a pointer to the actual location of the item on the network.

Depending on the item type, the user is given a choice of examination/browsing options. For example, text can be examined with a text editor, and scientific data sets can be examined using a number of data analysis tools. When the user chooses one of the tools, the interface automatically starts up the analysis tool for the user and informs the tool of the location of the data set. In the case of data generators, a choice of data analysis tools is given for use as the user interface for control and viewing of the process. Users can also elect to transfer a copy of the item to local disk; however, many examine options involve use of the item at its original location. The list of items can also be saved to local disk.

NETWORK ARCHITECTURES, PROTOCOLS, AND MULTIMEDIA DIGITAL LIBRARIES

The nature of access to the data in a multimedia digital library greatly affects the network architectures and protocols required. At the same time, network architecture and also resource billing schemes will determine what are the most cost-effective access methods and thus will affect the way users access data.

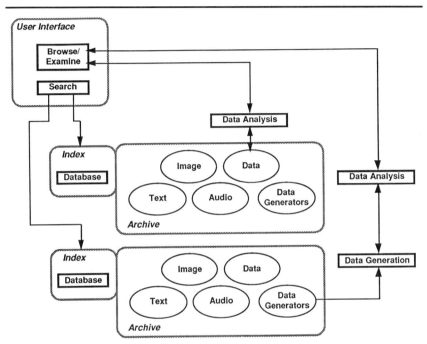

Figure 2. Model used to build the NCSA multimedia digital library prototype
(© 1991 Catlett, Terstriep)

For access to remote data over the network, existing Internet archives allow for limited browsing and examination of text (using bulletin boards) but only for retrieving most data (images, large text files, software) to local disk to examine or browse. The multimedia digital library must support remote access to data as many of the items will be too large for the amount of disk available locally to the user and many of the items will require access to facilities (e.g., supercomputers) that do not reside with the user.

To access data remotely without retrieving the data to local disk in total, a number of types of access can be supported. The popular Network File System (NFS) protocol from Sun Microsystems allows files on remote disk to appear as though they are on local disk. This is done by allowing the user to access the files in subunits (transparent to the user) called blocks. However, if the user only requires a particular record or byte (perhaps every nth byte), NFS still sends the data in blocks, and the subunits are extracted from the blocks by the user's workstation.

In some cases, it may be more suitable to allow the user's application to extract information from the remote file by individual bytes rather than blocks. In other cases, a user will want a whole group of items (e.g., files) to be sent to the local workstation so that they can be manipulated locally.

Each of these remote access methods—groups of files, whole files, blocks, bytes—dictates requirements on the network supporting the access. For example, where text or images are being browsed, the user should be able to "flip" through several pages per second. This may be most easily done by retrieving in total the entire file or group of files to be browsed. For image sequences, however, the entire image sequence may be too large to fit on the user's disk and must be accessed in parts. Images could be sent over the network in sequence, requiring isochronous, in-order delivery. In this case, lost or damaged images or portions of images will be better skipped than retransmitted. To provide isochronous viewing, groups of images could be sent over the network and played locally, with a number of images waiting to be viewed at the local workstation at any given time. This would allow the workstation to deliver the images at a constant rate, relaxing the requirement of the network to do so. In addition, a queue of images at the local workstation may provide enough time to retransmit lost or damaged images.

It is important to note that delivery of information at a constant rate in the presence of any errors will come at a cost of reliable delivery of all information. This is because error correction measures such as retransmission come at a cost of delays, and these delays may cause more disruption in the image stream than the error they are meant to correct in the first place.

When viewing a sequence of images, part of the information that is contained is the development of features in time. Thus delivery of the information at a rate that distorts the time element will deliver incorrect information to the user.

The billing algorithms of the network will also drive the way that the data are accessed. An example of this effect can be seen in the delivery of electronic mail. When mail is delivered using dial-up phone circuits such as with UUCP (UNIX-to-UNIX copy protocol), the cost of delivery is dependent upon a circuit setup cost and a time-sensitive usage cost. Therefore, to minimize the number of calls and the length of calls, electronic mail is queued and sent periodically. Internet mail delivery systems such as SMTP (simple mail transport protocol) assume that there is no cost to setting up circuits or in usage. Therefore, to minimize delay in mail delivery, each mail message is delivered as soon as it is submitted. The result is that Internet mail is much more interactive than UUCP because of the cost structure of the underlying network services rather than because of any technical considerations.

The current Internet cost structure is a fixed cost, not sensitive to usage. The fixed cost generally involves the cost of equipment at installation time, the cost of leasing telecommunications circuits, and some cost for maintaining an operations staff locally and/or at a central network operations center. In this environment, a multimedia digital library might download small items for local examination and access large items remotely. The difference between large and small will be determined by the capacity of the network, the amount of local storage space, and the amount of time the user is willing to wait while information is retrieved. With time-sensitive network connections such as a circuit-switched (dial-up, ISDN) connection, the trade-off will also include the cost of keeping the circuit up for large retrieval and the cost of keeping the circuit up for long sessions of remote data examination.

DATA GENERATORS: HIGH-PERFORMANCE APPLICATIONS

Several high-performance applications are described below. These applications have intensive network requirements. The multimedia digital library prototype described above allows users to access these types of applications; therefore, they must be taken into account in assessing the effect of multimedia digital libraries on a network.

Radio Astronomy

The Hat Creek radio telescope collects information at 2,048 frequencies. The telescope data must be converted into visual images using computational image-processing techniques. Supercomputers are used for this, acting as the image-forming element of the telescope. The conversion involves a calibration calculation to filter out much of the interference caused by atmospheric anomalies, then a FFT (Fast Fourier Transform) to convert the raw telescope output data into images. For each frequency, a two-dimensional image is produced. Thus the image output to a radio telescope is a spectral cube, with two spatial dimensions and one spectral dimension. In the case of the Hat Creek array, this cube is 2,048 frequencies by up to 4,096 horizontal and 4,096 vertical pixels with each pixel being 16 to 24 bits. For example, a 2,048 by 2,048 spatial size with 24 bits per pixel would involve the following amount of data:

2,048 frequencies • 2,048×2,048 pixels/frequency • 24 bits/ pixel • 1 byte/8 bits = ~26 gigabytes.

Reconstruction of these image cubes from the data requires real-time interaction by a scientist who observes roughly two to five images per second being displayed. Typically, one spectral image is used in this process, and the scientist will watch the image reconstruction as the nonlinear deconvolution either converges on an image or begins to diverge, indicating the need to stop the process and restart after adjusting gain parameters. Analysis of the resulting spectral cube involves traversing both the spatial dimensions and the spectral dimensions.

Data are collected continuously by the telescope and are integrated over time to increase the signal-to-noise ratio. The integration time, generally measured in tenths of seconds to tens of seconds, is determined as a function of the signal strength of the object being observed. Where very long integration times are used, the telescope would not necessarily be steered in real time. Short integration times are generally desired for real-time observation.

Several classes of observation require these images to be produced in real time for interactive steering of the telescope. The integration time would be on the order of tenths of seconds to several seconds. These classes include observation of time-variable phenomena such as solar activity, a technique called "mosaic-ing" (where short observations are made on a number of small regions and then reconstructed into a larger image later), and in cases where the atmospheric changes, which happen on the order of seconds, are kept to a minimum.

A prototype that was demonstrated by BIMA scientists at NCSA recently involved the functional decomposition of this type of system, using both the CRAY Y-MP for the baseline calculation and the massively parallel CM-2 for the FFT. By spreading the computation across several supercomputers, the speed of the computation increased significantly.

Atmospheric Sciences

Interactive visualization systems involve both analysis of precomputed data and analysis of running simulations. For the analysis of precomputed data, a supercomputer is used to render thunderstorm data using surfaces, contour plots, massive particle releases, and slices. The supercomputer simulation involves calculating the evolution of a weather system for a region of the atmosphere. For example, a region that is 100 km long by 50 km wide and 30 km high is subdivided into a grid of zones, each zone perhaps 1 km by 1 km by 500 meters. Several variables are associated with each of these zones, including temperature, pressure, and velocity vectors. The supercomputer simulation involves using the laws of physics to compute the evolution of these variables over a period of time from some beginning state. A typical simulation as described above has over 1 million zones, each with nine variables. The variables are stored in 8-byte fields, thus the amount of data required to represent one moment in the storm evolution is

~1,000,000 zones • 9 variables/zone • 8 bytes/variable = 72 megabytes.

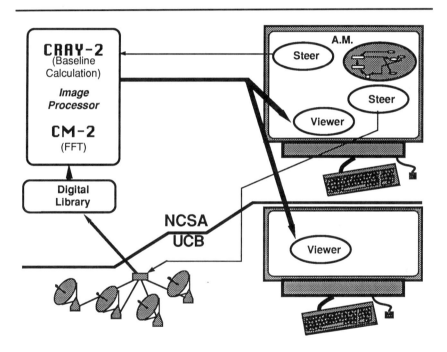

Figure 3. Prototype radio astronomy application that was developed using both the CRAY-2 and the CM-2 to interactively evaluate the frequency response of a given radio telescope antenna configuration

The resolution shown above, with each zone representing an area 1 km by 1 km by 500 meters, is not high enough to study small-scale phenomena such as tornados. In order to reduce the zone size for this scale of activity, the number of zones would increase beyond the capacity of any available supercomputer memory, and the amount of time it would take to calculate all of the variables for even a single moment in time would exceed the compute power of even the fastest current supercomputers. To address the need for higher resolution, interactive systems are being developed to allow the scientist to intervene in the running simulation and request a higher or lower resolution in portions of the simulated storm system. This will allow for increasing resolution in those areas with high activity without increasing the overall size of the simulation beyond feasible limits.

These types of applications are also being distributed over multiple computers to increase the computation rate. A current project involves the use of multiple RS/6000 workstations at NCSA to compute the model. Early studies have yielded a three-fold decrease in turnaround time when comparing one RS/6000 to using six in parallel, even for relatively small model sizes.

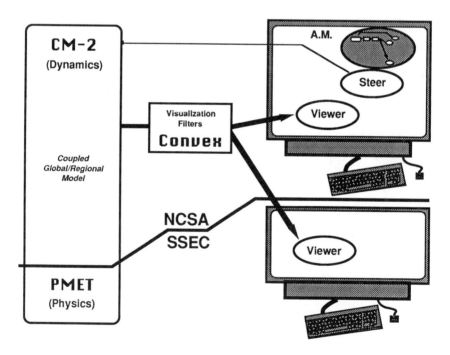

Figure 4. Coupled global/regional climate model using the PMET at Wisconsin and the CM-2 at Illinois

Biomedical Imaging

The Distributed Biomedical Imaging Laboratory (DBIL) is a testbed to integrate imaging instrumentation used in biomedical research with remote high-performance computing environments. DBIL is a joint project between NCSA and the University of Illinois Biomedical Magnetic Resonance Laboratory, with remote collaborators at Lawrence Berkeley Laboratories.

One application that has been demonstrated is the use of a CRAY-2 and CM-2 for 3D image reconstruction simultaneously during data acquisition from a nuclear magnetic resonance imaging spectrometer.

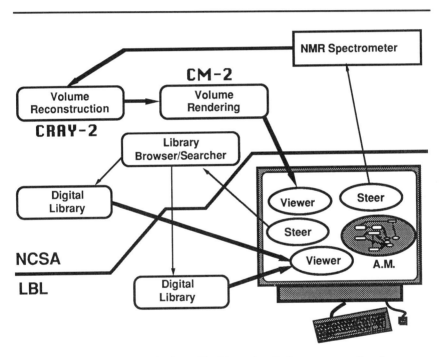

Figure 5. Distributed Biomedical Imaging Laboratory application

The reconstructed volumetric image is then sent to a CM-2 for volume analysis and visualization in a distributed display environment. The CRAY-2 image reconstruction takes roughly 0.05 seconds for each projection, and after one to one hundred projections are calculated, the volume of data (up to several megabytes) is sent to the CM-2. The processes run continuously for the duration of the experiment (10 to 60 minutes).

This original system allowed 3D rendering of a static image—a 3D snapshot. The system that has recently been demonstrated allows 3D rendering of a dynamic image—a 3D movie. Using this system, a frog egg will be observed over a 24-hour period to yield a 3D movie of cell multiplication.

REFERENCE

Smarr, L. L., & Catlett, C. E. (in press). Life after Internet: Making room for new applications. In B. Kahin (Ed.), *Building an information infrastructure.* New York: McGraw-Hill.

M. E. L. JACOB

M. E. L. Jacob Associates
Columbus, Ohio

Networking Applications
for Research Libraries*

ABSTRACT

This panel consisted of four speakers who are involved with a number of different network applications: Steve Cisler of Apple Computer, Clifford A. Lynch of the University of California at Oakland, Ward Shaw of the Colorado Alliance of Research Libraries (CARL), and Bernard G. Sloan of the Illinois Library Computer Systems Office (ILCSO). The panel was chaired by M. E. L. Jacobs and encompasses some eighty-two years of combined networking experience.

INTRODUCTION

Jacobs began the discussion by highlighting several themes that had been raised in preceding papers. Among these were how and why people communicate, public rights versus property rights, and where system boundaries are drawn.

How and Why People Communicate

Today we suffer information paralysis brought on by access to diverse sources of overlapping, redundant information, with little assistance to the user in identifying unique pieces of data or in sifting through

---

*This paper is a summary of the panel discussion titled "Networking Applications for Research Libraries."

99

the masses of data to locate either the best or, at least, the most appropriate piece for that particular purpose. We need to better understand why and how scholars and other information users communicate and how they seek and use information. Most scholars tend to ask one another, not use library and information centers, because it is easier. In addition, their colleagues will also provide a brief critique or analysis of the strengths and weaknesses of the research or of the researcher's methods.

Students, on the other hand, use libraries more, often want one or two relevant references, and are less concerned with the best references or the more exhaustive search. In other words, they want usable information immediately. Librarians and information professionals must suit their approach and the results sought to the needs of the requester; they must also be willing to take more responsibility in assessing information, in giving qualitative judgments, and in providing digested information instead of a list of articles or copies of all articles.

Public Rights versus Property Rights

Public rights and property rights must be balanced. Just because technology makes it easy to obtain copies and to manipulate data does not abrogate property rights of the individual or of the corporation. Public policy must find ways to continue to promote the unfettered exchange of information while at the same time encouraging innovation by providing economic incentives to creators and distributors of information. Networks must be able to offer both free services and commercial services and must provide adequate protection and recompense to each.

System Boundaries

The third aspect of networking applications, where system boundaries are drawn, can complicate solutions and end with suboptimal systems if the boundaries are drawn too narrowly. Information providers and information systems designers must look at the entire information cycle from creation through publication, distribution, storage, and retrieval to use and then to create further information. Looking only at publication and distribution may be ignoring other important consequences.

For example, why doesn't the Library of Congress Office of Copyright Deposit accept books in both print and machine-readable form? Almost all manuscripts today are produced via electronic typesetting. When a new edition is contemplated, the depository could provide the publisher and author with an electronic version of the manuscript. Too often today, a revision starts from scratch with the text rekeyed. Electronic manuscripts would also be an asset to scholars studying various writers and writing styles as well as book design.

THE SPEAKERS

Steve Cisler
Senior Scientist, Apple Computer Library

Cisler described the recent reorganization of Apple Computer and the place of the Apple Computer Library as part of the Advanced Technology Group. He also mentioned a number of projects outside Apple using Apple equipment. The University of Alaska, Fairbanks, has an oral history project to place data in digital form on CD-ROM. Project Jukebox will eventually provide access to these data via their network. North Carolina State University and the National Agricultural Library (NAL) are experimenting with sending images via the Internet as part of NAL's text digitizing project. Also described and demonstrated was some innovative software, WAIS (Wide Area Information Server) Station, for organizing and storing mixed media information developed by the staff of Thinking Machines Incorporated in Cambridge, Massachusetts, and made available free to researchers for experimentation.

Clifford A. Lynch
Director of Library Automation,
University of California at Oakland

Lynch described the University of California's use of that same software—WAIS Station—in an application that was up and operating in ten days. He also raised issues about some things libraries could be doing and were not.

For example, although most libraries now have online catalogs, few are available on or linked to the campus local area networks (LANs). Lynch emphasized that they should be. In a related example, electronic mail is an easy application to mount and use, yet few libraries have taken advantage of it to communicate with users. Search results could be mailed electronically instead of by campus mail or by forcing users to come to the library to pick them up. Printing has become a nightmare for many libraries, and soon, full text will increase printing demands. Lynch suggested working with departmental units or other campus resources to make hard-copy results available to users in their departments or dormitories. Ultimately, libraries should be able to deliver printed output over the campus LAN to the individual's workstation.

Another problem is authorization and resource control. Ensuring that only valid users have access to resources is not easy. Presently, users must obtain different cards and authorizations for different functions such as libraries, student unions, bookstores, and computers. In the case of limited resources such as high-quality color printers, how is access controlled and limited? With more network users, particularly remote users, questions of authorization and resource control will become critical.

Present network directories indicate what resources exist, but they do not provide much assistance in accessing them. This is an area where libraries and librarians could help. They should also consider providing systems that would supply full text along with citations if articles were located anywhere on the network.

Ward Shaw
President and CEO, Colorado Alliance of
Research Libraries (CARL)

Shaw suggested that name authority files are the place to carry authorizations. He then described the difference between CARL, a not-for-profit organization, and CARL Systems, a for-profit related corporation that markets and sells services developed by or for CARL. CARL has over 11 million bibliographic records, 4,500 terminals, and 175 databases as part of its online system available on the Internet. UNCOVER provides access to serials' tables of contents and is the third most popular CARL service. UNCOVER II, a full-text delivery service, will be introduced in summer 1991. Fax transmission will be used, and the bit-mapped images will be stored for later reuse. CARL Systems will pay royalty fees for articles delivered.

Shaw then raised two problems that occur when offering services: (a) whom to ask for permission and (b) whom to blame when things go wrong. Locating serials' publishers and obtaining permission to use serials' tables of contents have not been easy. Shaw indicated that, sometimes, it is easier to do something first and ask later. The second problem, troubleshooting, is also a major challenge in networked systems. Identifying the particular piece of equipment or line of software code responsible for a problem is not easy. Once the fault has been identified, the problem then becomes identifying who is responsible for fixing it. End-users need a lot of guidance in matching their needs to systems and equipment.

Local system vendors do not know a lot about connectivity. Although users talk about it, few really demand it or are willing to pay for it. Not all libraries want to be connected to networks. Some fear that users will demand too much, swamping existing systems, collections, and personnel. Others fear that inadequacies in these will become more apparent to users under networking.

Bernard G. Sloan
Director, Illinois Library Computer Systems Office (ILCSO)

Sloan described ILLINET (Illinois Library Network) Online, which provides an online catalog and circulation system for thirty-eight libraries: nineteen private colleges, thirteen state universities, four community colleges, one high school library, and the Illinois State Library. Some 1,400 terminals access the 20 million holdings on the system. Three hundred and seventy-two libraries use the system: 58 percent public, 22 percent academic, 13 percent school, and 7 percent special libraries. Seventy-five percent of the $4.3 million funding comes from the Illinois Board of Higher Education, 10 percent from the state library, and 15 percent from ILCSO. Connections to the Internet are planned, and introduction of the BRS workstation software is underway. Databases being considered are Wilson, Information Access Corporation, and University Microfilms Incorporated.

CONCLUSION

A lively discussion with the audience ensued with a number of questions on the software demonstrated by Steve Cisler. One participant suggested that libraries should allow users to annotate bibliographic records with notes. Another remarked that this feature was provided in the late 1960s and early 1970s by MIT's Project INTREX and that Carnegie-Mellon was using electronic mail to communicate with its online catalog users.

MARTIN RUNKLE

Director, University of Chicago Library
Chicago, Illinois

The Changing Economics of Research Libraries

ABSTRACT

This paper discusses, from the viewpoint of a library administrator, the economic and funding problems raised by the involvement of academic libraries in networks. With increased access to electronic information provided by networks, librarians must be involved with planning what will be available on the network. In addition, a structure is needed to facilitate collaboration among various members of the university community to manage the system. Given the development of electronic information technology and libraries' limited financial resources, librarians must budget for expenditures related to providing electronic information as well as expenditures related to providing access to traditional materials. Librarians will have to determine priorities, scrutinize budgets, and consider alternatives for reallocating money.

INTRODUCTION

The title of this paper was suggested by the title of Martin Cummings's (1986) book, *The Economics of Research Libraries*. This book was the result of a two-year effort that was organized by the Council on Library Resources and involved a number of people and some commissioned studies. Cummings asserted that "we know little about the economics of research libraries or the relationship of library budget decisions to the felt needs of users" (p. 12). Our knowledge of the economics of research libraries has not improved much since this book was published, and, in fact, the picture has become more complex.

104

A few years ago, the provost of the University of Chicago (UC) began a budget address to the faculty with the statement, "To budget is to choose." Though this is an exciting time for librarians, we are faced with very difficult budget choices. The choices center mainly on trying to maintain the traditional library while incorporating new information technology.

It is difficult to judge whether or not today's economic constraints are that much different from those of difficult periods in the past, but we are all familiar with what has been happening recently to the price of publications that are of interest to research libraries.

Figure 1 is taken from *ARL Statistics, 1989-90* (Stubbs, 1991, p. 6). The graph shows that median serials expenditures of ARL libraries rose 52 percent from 1986 to 1990. In the same four years, the median price per subscription rose 51 percent, while the median number of subscriptions decreased by only 1 percent.

For monographs, the numbers are even more troubling. In spite of a 19 percent increase in expenditures for monographs during this period, the number of monographs purchased dropped 16 percent. Serials were protected to a great extent at the expense of monographs, and libraries have been acquiring an increasingly smaller portion of what is being published. At the same time, patrons' expectations regarding access to traditional information sources have been rising, and the volume of interlibrary lending has increased dramatically.

INFORMATION TECHNOLOGY: PROMISES AND PROBLEMS

There are some truly exciting advances in information technology and the promise of networking—end-user access from offices and homes to a vast array of bibliographic, textual, numeric, and graphic information, as well as new forms of information structured in multidimensional ways previously not possible and approaching the metaphysical. One of the new developments is something called "virtual reality."

UC has not gone nearly as far as some other universities in providing access to electronic information through networking, but it is fairly typical. We have a high-speed campus network that is being extended to most campus buildings. It connects with external networks and is heavily used by some faculty and students. Although the library's online catalog is available on this network, except for law databases and what is freely available on the Internet, we do not provide end-user access to other databases on the campus network. Most faculty and students do not use the campus network because they are not familiar with its capabilities, and, besides, it is not very user-friendly.

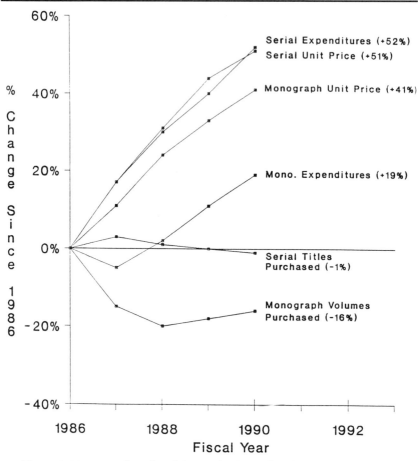

Figure 1. Monograph and serial costs in ARL libraries, 1985-86—1989-90

For the time being, most of the faculty and students do not know what they are missing. But that will soon change. As word spreads and as faculty and graduate students come to our university from other institutions that are ahead of us, the pressure will mount for us to do more, and we will be obliged to do more to remain competitive, as well as merely to do our jobs.

It is troubling to observe that an increasing number of students, and even faculty, at UC—and one must assume at other universities— are inclined not to use the card catalog. Their research is being shaped and limited by what they find in the online catalog. Even the most conscientious of scholars can drift onto the path of least resistance, and in order not to allow the past to be overlooked, research libraries must place a high priority on converting card catalogs to machine-readable form.

A similar phenomenon relates to electronic indexing and abstracting services when these databases contain entries only for recent years. As more textual and other information becomes available in electronic form, the trend toward regarding only relatively current information will become even more pronounced.

Though electronic information technology has moved at an amazing pace, publications distributed in traditional formats will be with us for a while, and university libraries will continue to manage these formats for the foreseeable future. As one grows older, it becomes easier and easier to predict with great assurance that certain things will not occur in one's lifetime. When the author visits his library's binding and labeling department and sees just one day's worth of the printed volumes that are acquired from all over the world, he knows that most of them will not be superseded by electronic formats in his lifetime. We are obligated to preserve these collections, build on them, and facilitate their use. Unfortunately, it will become increasingly difficult to do so as we divert more resources to new information technology.

WHO PAYS?

How have we been paying for the new technology up to now? Access to electronic information using video display screens was introduced in academic libraries in the mid-1970s and became common by 1980. Since the mid-1970s, academic library budgets have increased steadily. There have been studies that attempt to determine the effect of the increases in terms of actual purchasing power, but the conclusions are not definitive. Regardless of the actual value of the increases, they have been, on average, substantial both in percentages and in absolute dollars. Many academic institutions have stretched themselves to support their libraries.

The breakdown of expenditures of ARL libraries suggests some interesting trends in the past fifteen years. Even allowing for some inconsistencies in what has been included by libraries in the various categories, some trends are evident.

At the author's request, Kendon Stubbs updated a graph that originally appeared in the *1983/84 ARL Statistics* (Daval & Lichtenstein, 1985, p. 4). The updated graph shows the percentage of change in selected categories of ARL statistics for the fifteen years from 1976 through 1990. These data are for the ninety libraries that reported data in all fifteen years. Using 1976 as a base, the figures show the following changes:

Serials expenditures	325 percent
Other operating and binding expenditures	322 percent
Salaries and wages	169 percent
Nonserial acquisitions expenditures	156 percent
Volumes held	48 percent
Current serials received	16 percent
Total professional and nonprofessional staff	11 percent
Gross volumes added per year	-6 percent

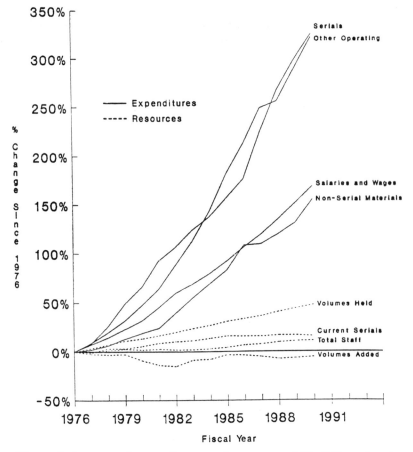

Figure 2. Aggregated expenditures and resources of 90 ARL university libraries, 1975-76—1989-90

The "other operating and binding expenditures" have increased at a much faster rate than total acquisitions or staff expenditures. As other people have suggested, it seems likely that the disproportionate growth of these other expenditures represents increases related to automation and access to electronic information—expenses such as equipment, licensing and user fees of various sorts, and telecommunications costs. If some libraries are paying some of such expenses from acquisitions budgets, the differences in the growth of the various categories are even greater than the graph shows.

Other added expenditures associated with providing electronic information are staff costs. These are for systems staff who are dedicated to providing the technology, as contrasted to staff who use the technology such as reference librarians and catalogers. These new staff undoubtedly account for some of the increase in staff size.

It is likely that some of the increase in library budgets in the past fifteen years has been earmarked for information technology by the parent institutions and would not otherwise have been allocated to libraries. It is also likely, however, that some money that would have gone to acquisitions budgets for traditional formats has gone to information technology instead. In other words, acquisitions budgets for traditional formats have been squeezed.

Not all expenditures for information technology are revealed in individual library budgets. State systems of higher education have funded systemwide capabilities. And in many institutions, the costs of library processing systems and of providing access to electronic databases have been at least partially supported through the budgets of university computing organizations or academic departments.

But what of the future? As we are faced with system replacement costs and as expectations, technical possibilities, and costs continue to rise, how are we going to pay for it all? Obviously, we cannot afford to pay for it all, and we will have to make choices.

THE "IDEAL" LIBRARY

Libraries are often described as bottomless pits. There seems no limit to the amount of money that could be spent on them, and this is because of the traditional ideal of an academic library—an ideal that never could be fully realized but that everyone wishes for, nevertheless. The following list suggests a few of the characteristics of the ideal library of twenty years ago—an ideal that for the most part is still held today.

- The time between publication of an item and its bibliographical and physical availability in the library should be as short as humanly possible.
- Catalog records should be thorough and accurate and have many access points.

- There should be several comprehensive catalogs, as well as smaller catalogs that are subject-specific.
- The catalogs should contain article-specific entries for journals.
- The library should be open 24 hours a day.
- There should be subject specialist librarians in all disciplines and languages to select materials for the collections and to help people find what they need.
- Reference desks and circulation counters should be open all the hours the library is open and should be sufficiently staffed so that people do not have to wait for service.
- When books are returned from circulation, they should be reshelved within minutes.
- Stacks should be kept in good order and shelf-read frequently.
- Lost, misplaced, or damaged materials should be replaced promptly.
- On those few occasions when something needed is not in the local collections, it should be retrievable from another library in a timely way, preferably within hours.
- All materials in the collections should be physically arranged by subject classification numbers. There should be multiple copies with different numbers when various class numbers apply to the item.
- The library should acquire all of the publications that might be needed for the university's programs of education and research, with at least two copies of each title so that one can be noncirculating and always available on the shelves. Additional copies should be made available when demand is expected to be heavy. For some disciplines, departmental libraries should contain a duplicate subset of what is in main libraries.
- There should be no microfilm. Everything should be in hard copy.

The point of this potentially infinite list is that there has always been a set of impossible standards that people have consciously or unconsciously used in judging a library. Libraries are always less than people wish them to be. The job of the librarian has been to negotiate compromises and to convince people that the compromises are reasonable, that financial resources are being spent wisely, and that the various constituencies are being fairly served. This job is becoming increasingly difficult.

Today's online library catalogs are coming closer to, and even surpassing, the ideal configuration of card catalogs that was fantasized twenty years ago. Electronic information and networking capabilities open up the possibility of someday achieving and even surpassing the other ideals in the list. The technology seems to be within reach, and we are all eager to make this possibility a reality. Our expectations are higher, and the gap between expectations and reality is even greater.

In making budget decisions, librarians have always had to consult widely and negotiate among competing, sometimes conflicting, demands. But the emergence of electronic information in a network environment has made it far more difficult to manage the decision-making process. Many of the historical precedents do not apply to our new environment, and, more than ever before, the decisions require broadly based deliberation and consultation within the institution, and the decisions also require accountability regarding the choices that are made. In many institutions, the political and economic path to changing over to an online catalog was a rocky and precarious one. The road to the electronic library will be even more treacherous.

PLANNING FOR THE NEW INFORMATION TECHNOLOGY

The terms *information technology* and *networks* have been used here rather loosely. Libraries began developing in-house automated circulation and processing systems in the late 1960s and gradually moved toward online catalogs for patron access. These systems are focused on managing the local collections and supporting the operations of the library. Planning the systems, securing the funding for them, and insuring that they are put in place and maintained are clearly the responsibility of the library.

The most appropriate assignment of responsibility for the various aspects of the campus network is less clear. One aspect of campus networks is the development and maintenance of the physical medium of communication and of the software that provides for the transmission of data and for connectivity, within the institution as well as to external networks. This aspect has been compared to building and maintaining a highway. Another aspect is the design and implementation of user-friendly interfaces and directories of capabilities and databases. A third aspect is the selection of electronic capabilities and databases that will be made available and the terms under which they will be made available to local constituents and to people not directly affiliated with the local institution.

Libraries have already assumed a leadership role and in some cases assumed financial responsibility for providing access to databases whose contents resemble traditional library information sources. The present CD-ROM versions of what were previously printed sources seem obviously the province of the library. Networked databases, however, whether mounted locally or available from remote locations, raise more complex issues and expenses.

As networks continue to be developed and the number of machine-readable databases grows, colleges and universities need structures for identifying options, determining priorities, and choosing among options for the allocation of resources, including making judgments about value and cost. The trade-offs required are too difficult and too politically sensitive to be managed in traditional ways. A structure is needed that provides collaboration among (a) faculty representatives of academic disciplines, (b) staff with expert knowledge of computer and communications capabilities and costs, and (c) librarians who understand the vast array of information that can be made available and the ways it might be used.

It is becoming increasingly important for librarians to be facilitators of decision making, as well as decision makers. They have a major role in identifying issues that must be addressed and in gathering and organizing the information needed to make decisions. Among the information that must be brought to bear on the decisions is the cost of providing information in both traditional and electronic formats. Most libraries do not invest enough money in collecting and analyzing management information. Because librarians are always so far from providing the ideal library, they are reluctant to divert money from activities that will directly and immediately improve services to users. One application of information technology that we should somehow fit into our budgets is the capacity for better cost accounting and the provision of other management information about our operations.

We must assume that income to colleges and universities cannot be expanded sufficiently to pay for everything we would like to do or feel obligated to do. Certainly, we need to continue to make the case and argue for funds. Certainly, institutions that are part of state systems should argue for funding for systemwide capabilities. And certainly, within institutions, librarians should try for cost sharing with other academic departments. But whatever the success of the efforts for funding, economies and trade-offs will have to be made.

Regardless of who controls the decisions and the budgets for networking and access to electronic information, these new capabilities will continue to compete with traditional library collections and services. We must continue to sharpen our priorities, scrutinize our budgets, and consider possibilities for reallocating money. Following are some possibilities for economies in the categories of (a) charging for services, (b) performing traditional services more efficiently, (c) reducing or eliminating traditional services, (d) reducing collecting in traditional formats, and (e) cooperation and resource sharing.

Charging for Services

As access to certain kinds of electronic information and networking capabilities becomes more the accepted norm and is considered a requirement, not a mere convenience or special service, we will be unable to establish a pricing structure and impose cost-recovery fees to support base-level services. Some faculty and students are willing and able to pay for convenience or for highly individualized service from their own pockets or from grant funds. However, it is firmly embedded in academic culture that the institution will provide access on a more or less equal basis to the basic information people need to pursue their research and education. Charging for access to information would be like asking individual faculty members to rent the classrooms they teach in. This is capitalism run amok. Again, not in our lifetimes are we likely to risk discouraging students from doing research by making them pay as they go for access to the information they need.

Performing Traditional Services More Efficiently

Librarians have always strived to perform services more efficiently. There probably are not substantial additional savings to be realized, but without continual questioning of why we perform certain processes and paying attention to how we do them, efficiency will inevitably decline. Automation was first introduced as a way of performing library processing more efficiently. It did allow libraries to do things better but not necessarily at less cost. In fact, automation has raised expectations and opened new possibilities, so that as the cost of computing and storage capacity has decreased, applications have expanded to more than offset potential savings. As the online catalog gets increasingly bigger and more inclusive, and searching and other interactive capabilities get more and more sophisticated, increasing amounts of storage and computing capacity are used up, necessitating ever more complex software applications and staff resources to maintain them.

Reducing or Eliminating Traditional Services

In addition to trying to be efficient, libraries constantly explore possibilities for reducing or eliminating traditional services. Martin Cummings (1986) bemoans repeatedly the lack of cost analysis of library operations and services. Such analysis is difficult for much of what libraries do, but we need better information about costs to help us make choices, including choices regarding new information technology. As technology advances, we need to reexamine some of the old targets for budget cutting and see them in a new context. Perhaps the convenience lost by closing a departmental library could be more than offset by a new kind of convenience.

There are limits, however, to how far we can go in measuring and quantifying the benefits of libraries in general and the particular services they provide or the values that they represent. Academic libraries exist to support the goals and missions of their institutions. How can one establish a dollar value or do a cost-benefit analysis of much of the research and education that takes place in academic institutions?

Reducing the Level of Collecting in Traditional Formats

Can we consider offsetting the cost of electronic information by cutting back on acquisitions in traditional formats? In a sense, academic libraries have already reduced their level of collecting in traditional formats in that they are collecting an ever smaller portion of what is available to collect. Is there a realistic possibility of choosing to reduce the present level of acquisitions budgets by 25 percent or some other substantial amount? A reduction in acquisitions would also result in a reduction in the costs of processing and of space, though costs of providing access to other collections might increase.

Libraries have been reluctant to give up the printed versions even of sources that they are acquiring in electronic form, such as bibliographies and indexes on CD-ROM. Giving up the printed versions, although not encouraged by present pricing structures, would produce savings, but libraries have been concerned about losing ownership and being at the mercy of producers.

A particularly interesting example of the ownership issue is the extensive full-text literature in the field of law and on a broad range of other subjects that is available through LEXIS, NEXIS, and WESTLAW. The UC law librarian estimates that these databases contain the texts of over 97,000 of the volumes in the Law Library, which is 18 percent of its entire collection. Of the 12,500 volumes added to the Law Library last year, approximately 30 percent, or 4,000 volumes, are in these databases. All UC Law School faculty and students now have access to these databases from homes and offices, as well as from terminals in the Law Library, with no contractual limit on the amount of text they can print. All of this access is made available at unrealistically low rates because the vendors want law students to become dependent on these resources so that, when they go into practice, they will continue to use them but pay full freight. It will be interesting to see if use of the print collections in the UC Law Library declines sharply in the next year or two; it probably will.

We have not yet been able to bring ourselves to eliminate the printed versions of what is covered in these databases; we are concerned about becoming dependent on the electronic versions and vulnerable to greatly increased costs in the future. What happens if the vendors decide that these databases have become so firmly established and indispensable that they no longer need to offer such attractive rates to libraries, and we are suddenly faced with paying hundreds of thousands of dollars to continue the access we have had? Theoretically, we could revert to using only the printed forms of the publications, but realistically, can we? Once accustomed to the convenience and superior access of the electronic format, will faculty and students tolerate a return to access only to the printed form? Probably not—particularly not lawyers!

There is a clear danger that, if for-profit producers of electronic information acquire a monopoly or near monopoly on information in electronic form, we could face even worse profiteering than we now face with a few publishers of science journals. Although some people have predicted that further development and expansion of the publication of electronic journals will help us to address the high cost of journals, the economics are not so clear. Perhaps the effect of electronic journals will be like that of library automation: Enhance access immeasurably but not save money.

Resource Sharing

Libraries have for many centuries looked to cooperation and resource sharing as a way of fulfilling their missions. There were union catalogs of manuscripts long before the invention of printing (Richardson, 1936, p. v), and it is likely that groups of monasteries coordinated their copying of manuscripts.

Academic administrators see cooperation and resource sharing as a way of saving money. Librarians, on the other hand, see it as a way of expanding the information sources that can be made available to their constituencies, but not necessarily as a way of saving money. By cooperating, librarians can provide information and services that they could not otherwise provide.

The primary manifestation of resource sharing is the sharing of access to collections—on-site or by way of interlibrary lending. Access to collections held elsewhere is becoming increasingly important. Sharing of collections does not necessarily involve coordination of acquisitions among libraries. It can be merely the sharing of whatever materials libraries happen to have collected in trying to satisfy local needs. Although there has been a fair amount of informal coordination of acquisitions among libraries, we have been less successful with larger, more structured, and more formal programs. (An important exception is the Center for Research Libraries.)

We should try to do a better job of coordinating acquisitions among groups of libraries to insure that, collectively, we provide the broadest possible range of collection resources. Networking and information technology are providing mechanisms for improved coordination, and access through networks to the order files of other libraries is already affecting acquisitions decisions. Implementation of serials control systems in more libraries will provide the kind of specific and current information that is needed for better coordination of serials acquisitions. We should continue to reexamine the possibilities for coordination as networking and information technology improve.

At the same time, we should continue to improve even more the timeliness and reliability of interlibrary lending. To improve it to the level it should be, we must begin to think of it more as a business proposition and not as a moral issue or a test of altruism. The costs of borrowing or lending an item or providing photocopies through interlibrary loan are not trivial. Aside from fees that lending libraries might charge, the average cost of an interlibrary loan transaction is at least $8 on each end of the transaction, and some cost studies indicate it is $15 or $20. At $8, which is probably low, the cost of 10,000 interlibrary loan transactions is $160,000. It is puzzling that most libraries bury these costs in various parts of their budgets.

First, libraries should understand the costs of borrowing for their patrons and budget for it as a service. Second, lenders should be compensated for their costs. Most libraries will expedite lending transactions only if they are not losing money for their efforts and detracting from their local priorities. These points bear emphasizing because it is only by being more businesslike about interlibrary lending that we can maintain and improve the sharing of collections and provide the basis for more refined coordination of collection development. Access in place of ownership does not mean access without cost. It is possible that all the money now spent on interlibrary lending and borrowing could pay for a superior document delivery service on a very different model. We will not know this until we face up to the true costs of the present system.

There is also room for cooperation and sharing in the provision of electronic information, but, as with print collections, we must not assume, and base our planning on the assumption, that we can share freely without regard to cost. Producers of electronic information have a legitimate concern about recovering the costs of producing it, whether they are in the for-profit or not-for-profit sector. As with interlibrary lending, if external use of locally supported databases and other electronic information capabilities interferes with local use, owners of the resources will not be forthcoming in allowing access unless they are compensated.

CONCLUSION

This paper has not been able to address the economics of providing access to networking capabilities and electronic information as fully and specifically as the author would have liked. It has merely alluded to what everyone knows: it will cost more money than we can see our way clear to provide. The day when a scholar can sit at a workstation and have the entire world of information, or even a substantial portion of it, available at the click of a mouse or a voice command is a long way off. On our way to this day, we have some interesting cultural, technical, and economic issues to wrestle with. We will be required, as J. Warren Haas put it, "to make fundamental changes in the very definition of what a library is and to recast operations and services in a dramatically different mold" (Cummings, 1986, p. 7). Those of us in the business of recasting that mold are privileged to have such challenging and interesting jobs, but we have difficult choices ahead of us.

REFERENCES

Cummings, M. M. (1986). *The economics of research libraries.* Washington, DC: Council on Library Resources.

Daval, N., & Lichtenstein, A. (Comps.). (1985). *ARL statistics, 1983-84.* Washington, DC: Association of Research Libraries.

Richardson, E. C. (1936). Introduction. In A. Berthold (Comp.), *Union catalogues: A selective bibliography* (pp. v-xii). Philadelphia: Union Library Catalogue of the Philadelphia Metropolitan Area.

Stubbs, K. (1991). Introduction. In S. M. Pritchard and E. Finer (Comps.), *ARL statistics, 1989-90.* Washington, DC: Association of Research Libraries.

KENNETH R. R. GROS LOUIS

Vice President and Chancellor
Indiana University
Bloomington, Indiana

The Real Costs and Financial Challenges
of Library Networking: Part 1*

ABSTRACT

Library networking has created a number of administrative and policy issues. Questions of governance, budgeting, cooperation, and reporting lines must be addressed. In some cases, these issues must be addressed by librarians; in others, by campus administrators. In any event, the importance of the research library must be recognized, and support for the library's priorities must be marshalled.

INTRODUCTION

This conference touches on themes of major importance to each of us involved in higher education—governance, budgeting, cooperation, reporting lines. These issues, although difficult in themselves, become even more difficult when most schools face fiscal problems and when there is pressure to take advantage of recent technological advances. Administrative and policy concerns raised at this conference will be the subject of discussions at our home campuses for months, probably years, to come.

---

*This paper summarizes comments made by the author as part of a panel discussion titled "The Real Costs and Financial Challenges of Library Networking." Panel participants included Kenneth Gros Louis, Paul Hunt, Thomas Shaughnessy, and William Studer.

As the chief executive of the Bloomington campus of Indiana University (IU) and as chair for the past four years of the Committee on Institutional Cooperation (CIC), I have been involved with these concerns and how they will increasingly influence the future of research libraries. I am not a technological expert; instead my role at this conference is to look at some of those administrative and policy matters that inevitably come to mind when we examine cooperative programs of any kind.

GOVERNANCE

All universities, of course, have a long and good tradition of collegial decision making—of bottom-up planning. But I feel that the issues linked to the kinds of cooperation discussed at this conference are so diverse, so new, require such a variety of levels of expertise, and carry such enormous financial implications that some new paradigm will be necessary if we are to plan imaginatively and successfully for large-scale national arrangements that protect the resources we have been asked to preserve and that our faculty expects us to make available. In all this, it is likely that a tension will arise between those models of governance most of us are long accustomed to—not that any of them is poor or inefficient—and the growing fear that they may not be equal to the task ahead.

Certain questions are obvious and indeed have already been touched on. Some of them librarians will be answering; others chief academic officers will be answering. It may be useful to make the distinction about who will be doing what. Consider some of the questions:

1. What technologies and communication systems will be necessary in the future?
2. What features are needed to make library automation networks compatible?
3. How useful are retrieval tools to the average user, and who will be the average user?
4. Who will control access to stored information?
5. Who will determine standards, and how will they be arrived at?
6. Does increased participation in networks mean significant changes in service priorities?
7. What are the implications for each of you?

The list, of course, goes on. My own experience with the Center for Research Libraries and more recently as a member of the Commission on Preservation and Access has underlined for me that much of the current national organization structure of libraries, however successful, still remains enormously complicated, complex, intricate, hierarchical, and mysterious. At times, membership and participation seem to depend on relatively few people at each institution, and the ability to effect national change seems increasingly limited. All of the many acronyms that define who you are and what you do mean a lot, I realize, but the acronym is not always easy to get, and the multiple acronyms sometimes confound and confuse rather than clarify.

From my perspective, it is unlikely that the current models will be appropriate for any successful planning that will lead to national networked systems. I cannot imagine what organization will make budgetary and policy decisions for multiple institutions. I cannot imagine any of the existing administrative structures responsibly taking on these issues. I cannot imagine large research libraries preserving their collections to provide access to smaller libraries, nor can I envision smaller libraries giving up a good deal of their autonomy to become in a real sense branches of larger libraries.

These are the problems that must be addressed by librarians. The kinds of issues that provosts and chief academic officers must address involve the competition between the library of the future and other priorities of our institutions. Even now, as you all well know, the establishment of priorities is difficult, often puzzling. And not only will we face competing internal objectives, we must also be aware of external forces—state and federal agencies, local political interests, regional concerns, alumni, and the citizenry at large. I am not sure that we will be able to marshal the political forces necessary to gain the support needed. Think about other issues affecting us and requiring the same marshalling of the same forces: How often can they be called upon?

BUDGETING

Brett Sutton, Charles Davis, Jim Neal, and others have described to me the issues as they perceive them. In their letters and conversations, I have been struck by the similarity, at times the repetition, of certain words, certain phrases—networks, open and public access, distributed library, integration, community, communication, interconnections, collaboration—all suggestive of cooperation in ways that we have never seen before in American higher education.

I think of the most recent meeting of the CIC on March 18, 1990, in which the chief academic officers agreed that the fiscal crises now facing most of us are unlikely to be alleviated in the years ahead. We believe that public higher education will not fare well in debates at the state and national levels, that sentiment for raising taxes will not grow, that other demands on state and federal funds will increase, and that concerns about what we do with our resources will increasingly be central to a growingly suspicious public. How can we do more with the same dollars, or perhaps with fewer?

COOPERATION

That is the context, it seems to me, in which we must consider future scenarios, and in which we must realize that what we do may need to go far beyond what we have done or even imagined doing. The issue may not be the saving of particular traditions or even particular institutions; rather it may be a matter of preserving national resources. The CIC, for example, has been considering academic programs at each of our campuses. How many exotic programs should be offered in the Midwest? Is it possible for us to work cooperatively so that only two or three institutions offer certain programs? If we do not work cooperatively, is not there a danger that in the next decade or two it will turn out that no one in the Midwest has a program in some small enrollment area or, perhaps as bad, that half of the institutions in the region have such a program? It seems to us that only by pooling resources, not our resources but those of the nation, can we fulfill what the public, sometimes without knowing it, really expects of us.

As I cannot imagine universities doing business as usual in the next several decades, so too I cannot imagine libraries doing business as usual. I understand how enormously complex it will be for regional libraries to cooperate in collection development, resource sharing, perhaps even personnel sharing. I do not know how to do it, I am not sure it can be done, but I do believe that responses of academic officers, faculty budgetary advisory committees, and university presidents will be much more favorable if the level of cooperation among libraries is greater than it has been in the past. The real challenge is how to enhance collections with an existing or even shrinking budget by sharing collection development policies as well as databases and other means of accessing material. Ownership, like the ownership of some exotic degree program, must be abandoned in favor of access.

There are other concerns. I am not confident that integrated networks and greater cooperation will necessarily lead to better services for students and scholars. I am not even confident that such collaboration will lead to financial savings. The costs involved go well beyond the obvious investments in hardware and software and buildings, beyond the cost of staff recruitment and training.

Perhaps the issue of governance is the largest one we face. If each of us does participate in elaborate networks with other libraries, who will bear the initial costs? The major research libraries cannot by themselves carry the burden for everyone else. I suspect that the federal government might be willing to bear a good portion of the burden if members of Congress could be persuaded, as they have been on the issue of brittle books, that a truly national effort was underway to enhance collections for students and scholars in a coherent, coordinated plan that identified specific sites for certain collections, the mode of access to those collections for others not at that site, and in ways that radically altered the nature of libraries and the role of librarians.

REPORTING LINES

If the previous issue is complex, equally so is the issue of control of information on a single campus. Who will be in charge? Librarians? Those in administrative or academic computing? Those in telecommunications? Even if that decision is made locally, what happens at regional, indeed national, levels? If there are individual czars and czarinas on campuses, can or should the library community identify such individuals for regions as well?

CONCLUSION

I always come back to the questions surrounding the process of resource allocation. At Indiana, Jim Neal, our dean of libraries, participates as a member of my campus cabinet, attends staff and dean's meetings, and is involved in the setting of campus priorities. We now face a reduction from the state for the first time in fifty years, and as we consider our basic priorities, I am pleased to say that library support has risen to the top of the list. That speaks well for Jim, for the faculty confidence in him and his staff, but also for the value that faculty and staff place on the research library. We need to tap that support, understand it, explain to it what it is we believe needs to be done, marshal and organize it, and bring it to the attention of our state legislators and members of Congress.

THOMAS W. SHAUGHNESSY

University Librarian
University of Minnesota
Minneapolis, Minnesota

The Real Costs and Financial Challenges of Library Networking: Part 2*

ABSTRACT

The development of the virtual electronic library and the resulting shift in emphasis from ownership to access raise questions about the responsibility for local collection development. However, access depends on ownership; a network does not create new resources, it facilitates the sharing of existing resources. This sharing has resulted in burdensome levels of interlibrary loan activity. In addition to the financial costs that result from this activity, convenience costs to local users at the lending library and increased preservation costs must be considered. Finally, research libraries will not only be measured by ownership statistics but by access criteria as well, and they will also have to deal with the politics of virtual libraries and networking.

THE VIRTUAL (OR LOGICAL) LIBRARY AND NETWORKING

One of the most dangerous ideas to confront research librarianship in recent years is the notion of the virtual electronic library. This is the library represented in part by the OCLC and Research Libraries

---

*This paper summarizes comments made by the author as part of a panel discussion titled "The Real Costs and Financial Challenges of Library Networking." Panel participants included Kenneth Gros Louis, Paul Hunt, Thomas Shaughnessy, and William Studer.

Information Network (RLIN), plus the online public access catalogs (OPACs) of individual libraries, plus a vast array of commercial databases. So what is so dangerous about this idea? The danger is that it relieves libraries, in the minds of campus decision makers, of the responsibility to build local collections, to request more space for old-fashioned, paper-based collections, and to engage in all of the labor-intensive inventory control activities that are required by print collections. The so-called library without walls, however, continues to be very much a series of physical places housed within some very real walls. For it is these institutions that supply a great deal of the information requested via the networks.

The recent shift in emphasis from ownership to access—thinking that seems to have pervaded even our own field without much challenge—leads one to ask why any library should buy any print material at all. In fact, why even have a library? Would not an office equipped with fax machines, text-digitizing equipment, scholarly workstations, and other electronic telecommunication devices suffice? But what would such a center be providing access to? The answer rests heavily upon collections and other resources identified, selected, purchased, cataloged, processed, shelved, and made available for use by some library, somewhere, which invested in the ownership of scholarly material. In the last analysis, access depends on ownership.

Some have tried to compare research libraries to supercomputing centers. A relatively small number of supercomputers are sufficient to meet the needs of most academic researchers. Most of the university-based supercomputers have excess capacity, and consequently time on these machines is being sold to the private sector. But there are no "superlibraries." Most research libraries are able to acquire less than one-tenth of the world's publications each year (estimated by UNESCO to be some 850,000 titles).

It is also important to remember a statement that Dick DeGennaro made about networks: by itself, a network creates no new resources; it merely facilitates the sharing of existing resources. To build on DeGennaro's insight, one can compare the relationship between networks and libraries to the relationship between the musicians in an orchestra and their conductor: Networks, like batons, make no sound. The sounds that bring us to the concert hall and elevate our spirits are those made by the individual instrumentalists and virtuosos. We need to value and reinvest in our virtuoso library collections and move away from a situation in which we seem to know the cost or price of everything and the value of nothing.

USE OF NETWORKS—RESOURCE SHARING

The second topic briefly addressed here is one of the specific uses made of networks: resource sharing. In the past three years, interlibrary loan lending among the ten largest public academic research libraries increased by 16 percent, while borrowing increased by 25 percent. Reasons for less interlibrary loan activity among the largest are (a) overload, (b) internal tactics by staff to reduce workload, (c) fees, and (d) saying "no." Among all (large and small) Association of Research Libraries (ARL) university libraries, lending activity increased by 25.6 percent (1987-90), while borrowing increased by 30.5 percent. These one hundred or so university libraries loaned or borrowed more than 4.2 million items in 1989-90. If this rate of increase persists, by 1995-96, interlibrary transactions will increase to 6.3 million items. According to Rowland Brown, OCLC's former CEO, U.S. ARL libraries provide approximately 22 percent of the loans on OCLC but account for only 2.5 percent of the membership.

Tom Waldhart (1985), in his review article on interlibrary loan, postulates that if the volume of interlibrary loan activity were to approach just 5 percent of every library's total circulation, "it is highly unlikely...that the nation's libraries, or its interlibrary loan system, could effectively deal with numbers of this magnitude without a major breakdown in operation" (p. 217).

But the fact is that many of our libraries are already finding it impossible to keep up with existing levels of interlibrary loan traffic. As George Keller (1983) noted in his book, *Academic Strategy*, where pressures are in charge, the present gets attention, not the future; fighting brush fires and improvisation take precedence, not planning; defense is the game, not offense (p. 75).

Many of us believe that there are two driving forces behind the rising demand for resource sharing: the increased bibliographic access provided by OPACs and CD-ROMs and the use of resource sharing networks to borrow not just esoteric or seldom-used material but basic, curriculum-related undergraduate books and journals. We know this is happening in Minnesota, and it is probably occurring in other states as well. Because all of Minnesota's public colleges have converted their bibliographic records, it is possible to determine the age of library collections based on date of publication. Twenty-seven percent of the titles owned by these libraries were published before 1960; 26 percent were published in the 1960s; 27 percent in the 1970s; and 19 percent in the 1980s. One of these state university libraries currently has a listing of 450 journals from which it has requested the maximum number of photocopies allowable under the copyright law. A large and growing proportion of the 600 items that the University of Minnesota libraries lend each day is not research material. Not long ago, at a meeting similar to this one, Sheila Dowd, who was then head of collection development at Berkeley, said that the jury is still out on how far we can go in sharing materials that are central to our respective universities' missions.

COSTS OF NETWORKING/RESOURCE SHARING

Strange as it may sound, it is very difficult to get a handle on the costs of resource sharing. The Research Libraries Group (RLG) tried to conduct a study of these costs in five libraries in 1988 and came up with these figures: borrowing costs ranged from $13 to $20 per item; lending costs ranged from $5 to $15. If we were to assume that the average cost of an interlibrary loan transaction in 1990 was $15, then the ARL university libraries spent $63.6 million on this activity in 1989-90. This is almost three times the amount these libraries spent on binding and is 87 percent of the amount they spent for part-time student assistants. In just five or six years, if present trends continue, ARL university libraries could be spending 100 million dollars on interlibrary lending and borrowing.

There are obviously other costs in addition to financial ones. These include convenience costs to local users (to what extent is access like justice: is access delayed or denied?) and preservation costs (to what extent is the life span of library collections—particularly bound journals—being shortened due to repeated photocopying?). To the best of the author's knowledge, these costs have never been factored into the real costs (mushy as they are) of resource sharing.

MEASUREMENTS, STANDARDS, AND POLITICS

A few words about each of these. Measurement: We all bemoan the fact that research libraries continue to be measured according to ownership statistics—that bigger is necessarily better—and that quantity is synonymous with quality. Library volume counts; volumes added and serials subscribed to are simply inputs to the library organization. We need these measures, but we also need to measure "units of access." But as the ARL Committee on Statistics learned, trying to measure access is like trying to climb a very slippery slope. And while we may criticize the ARL statistics, they remain the best in the library world and continue to be relied upon by library administrators and other campus decision makers. Our challenge is to come up with valid access measures that focus on user outcomes, measures that balance our traditional measures of library inputs or throughputs.

With regard to standards, many librarians are far more interested in standards such as Z39.50 than they are in ACRL standards that state the responsibility of all academic libraries to develop collections that support the curriculum. There is no substitute for basic, up-to-date collections available on site. We would not think of borrowing basic laboratory equipment such as microscopes and Bunsen burners from another institution. Certain library collections are just as basic.

Finally, the politics of virtual libraries and networking must be considered. In many ways, the problems faced by libraries are similar to those of the health industry. In both areas, costs are escalating beyond our ability to keep pace, and questions of institutional responsibility are being raised—along with questions of access, the quality of services rendered, and the need for cost containment. One writer has suggested that research libraries are imprisoned by the book, and were they able to eliminate entirely the need to acquire and manage large print collections, up to 80 percent of the cost of operating these libraries might be saved or redirected. But the challenge that we face is managing our libraries over a fairly extended transition period. We are caught between two very different worlds. Many library administrators are trying to move towards a library without walls as they deal with resources that are very much placebound. But in the last analysis, most of us would acknowledge that Jim Penrod was right when he said that in the world in which we now live, capital and/or human resources or book collections can no longer guarantee success. Rather, he said, service quality, speed of response, and innovation are now the determinants of success in information organizations.

We need, therefore, to appreciate the fact that a great deal of the world's information continues to exist in print and paper. Consequently, for quite a few more years we will continue to need *real* libraries, not virtual ones.

REFERENCES

Keller, G. (1983). *Academic strategy: The management revolution in American higher education.* Baltimore, MD: Johns Hopkins University Press.
Waldhart, T. J. (1985). I. Performance of interlibrary loan in the U.S.: A review of research. *Library and Information Science Research, 7*(3), 209-229.

WILLIAM J. STUDER

Director, Ohio State University Libraries
Columbus, Ohio

The Real Costs and Financial Challenges of Library Networking: Part 3*

ABSTRACT

The development of electronic networks is seen by some as a way to lower the high costs associated with collecting, maintaining, and storing traditional print-based library material. In reality, at least for the near future, libraries will be faced with double costs associated with the storage of dual formats. Additional costs will also result from the need to inform and train potential users. And as users are exposed to a wider variety of relevant materials held at other libraries, interlibrary loan activity will increase with resulting increased costs associated with staff time, computer equipment and support, and network use. Finally, as a result of increased networking, a structure to coordinate resources and access will have to be developed.

ELECTRONIC NETWORK RESOURCES

The vast array of resources now made available through information and network technologies is rapidly outpacing our ability to facilitate users' optimum use of them. There are now some 200 online public access catalogs (OPACs) available on the Internet, a handful of bona

---

*This paper summarizes comments made by the author as part of a panel discussion titled "The Real Costs and Financial Challenges of Library Networking." Panel participants included Kenneth Gros Louis, Paul Hunt, Thomas Shaughnessy, and William Studer.

fide electronic journals, a growing amount of full-text materials, hundreds of topical bulletin boards and listservers, and literally countless other resources. How much awareness and use expertise do our academic communities have relative to these resources and accompanying access technology?

Not very much, it would seem. So, the challenge is to establish and maintain instructional programs (a collaborative effort between computing centers and libraries) to bring resource awareness to the user community and to inform specifically in access technology and methodology. For the research library, this will require a major and costly extension of involvement in the training function. During the 1990s, libraries simply must become a major source of education and training for use of electronic information networks.

At the same time, the production of print-based information will slacken only slightly, and the obligation to maintain and serve the millions of print volumes now populating our libraries will remain. So, once again, we are faced with add-on costs for additional functions, i.e., we will not be able to recover significant budget resources from the cessation or lessening of more traditional library services in order to reallocate to this greatly increased training role.

In terms of acquisition of information resources, the evolutionary development of the National Research and Education Network (NREN) and associated technologies will certainly be conducive to greatly increased electronic publishing, thereby giving libraries another cost center with which to cope, both in terms of acquisition or use costs and in terms of cataloging (and possibly storage) costs. This electronic format of information will not in any dramatic way substitute for print in the near future—all the associated costs for which will remain. There are only added costs when electronic-based information essentially supplements rather than supplants print-based information.

However, as we look to an eventual significant transition from print to electronic publishing, there is a potential cost-savings implication for libraries relative to storage and building expansion—assuming, of course, some form of reasonable central storage of electronic information of guaranteed archival quality. Most of a library's inexorable need for physical growth is related to the storage of bulky print volumes.

Electronic full-text publications, together with original print formats converted to electronic versions, represent a relatively minuscule portion of a library's overall information resources at the moment, but growth will likely be considerable and on an accelerating curve over the next ten years. Yet no one seems to be dealing realistically with the issue of archiving this electronic data, which will certainly incur substantial costs as volume and complexity grow.

INTERLIBRARY LOAN COSTS

Access to electronic information sources, both those locally available and those obtained over regional and national networks (including OPACs), has greatly increased many users' exposure to a wider variety of relevant materials, only a portion of which any given library will hold. Hence, costly interlibrary loan (ILL) traffic has increased almost exponentially. And we are only on the front edge of this demand, given the relatively few who are currently plugged into networked information sources. At Ohio State University (OSU), for instance, the number of requests to borrow materials from other libraries has risen 565 percent in five years. This rapid growth parallels a marked decline in the number of materials acquired locally. With reference to users' discovery of more and more relevant material via network access, it will also become more compelling to devise systems for direct request and receipt of the materials versus the cumbersome mediated ILL processes currently in place.

A significant network cost advantage in resource sharing derives from the capability to transmit fax over the Internet free of out-of-pocket telecommunications charges. A majority of ILL traffic consists of journal articles which can be transmitted via fax very cost-effectively with concomitant great improvement in timeliness of delivery.

As users take more and more advantage of access to network-based information resources, there will surely be more demand at local levels from "external" users who need assistance in using given databases—perhaps OPACs most of all. This will likely cause some tension in maintaining a balance of how much time and resource one devotes to helping external users while not diminishing service to the local constituency.

NETWORK CONNECTIVITY COSTS

Networking is unquestionably a force for good, but it also seems to embody the momentum of a revolutionary transformation. Speaking strictly of internal library settings, all staff want and need network connectivity—for user benefit, to be sure, but also very much for their own use of electronic mail, bulletin boards, and other resources. OSU Libraries finds itself in a few short years with 156 personal computer workstations in addition to terminals connected to our OPAC. Beyond the obvious purchase cost, this equipment requires installation, telecommunications/network connections, maintenance, repair, software upgrades, troubleshooting of all kinds, and eventual replacement. All of this means significantly increased add-on costs for which we have not been funded, but which somehow must be accommodated. Also, when full text with graphics comes more to the fore, we will need more expensive hardware to store and display images.

On a more mundane note, the cost of computer printer paper is a major one. How many people read the bulk of electronic information online? Most people print out reams, and so do users of public terminals with printers available free of charge. Ironically, the vast quantity of printer paper being consumed in the cause of electronic information dissemination represents a large and almost entirely add-on cost.

The labyrinth of networks forming the Internet are currently usable free of charge to end-users, but as the NREN evolves and government subsidies decline, will users (and libraries) be expected to pay some of the costs? Such a new and perhaps considerable cost obligation could pose a real barrier to use. Related is the issue of inevitable access restrictions to networks and/or to given databases, which will necessitate the creation of complex systems for authentication and even billing.

CONCLUSION

The decentralized and distributed virtual library is an exciting concept, certainly made more realizable through the connectivity networking provides. But it is also a worrisome construct made even more so when coupled with glib notions of immediate impacts of electronic publishing. Without some degree of collection development planning and coordination (for which the nation as a whole is likely too large a planning arena), the efficacy of the virtual library can readily break down because fewer and fewer libraries may acquire what more and more users need. This approach to resource sharing is very tempting and captivating to some university administrators who perceive library cost savings while at the same time wondrously making even more resources available to users. This author, for one, is very intrigued and interested but also very concerned with how to superimpose structure on such a free-form system. Relative to electronic publishing, there is a tendency on the part of some unschooled administrators to believe that the electronic information era has arrived and signals significant cost savings for libraries when, in fact, living with the double costs of dual formats will be the order of the day for some time to come.

CARL R. GRANT

Vice President of Marketing
Data Research Associates
St. Louis, Missouri

DRANET: An Information Network*

ABSTRACT

Data Research, a library automation firm, is also a database provider and the implementors and administrators of a nationwide library network called DRANET. Mounted on this network are the Library of Congress machine-readable cataloging (LCMARC) database (some 4 million records), Information Access Co. (IAC) indexes, and other library bibliographic files. LCMARC authority files and full text for selected serials will be added soon.

INTRODUCTION

DRANET was originally a bibliographic network, but it is rapidly changing in nature and is becoming, instead, an information network. This network links every type of library from grade schools to community colleges to four-year colleges and research libraries. Furthermore, DRANET is a node on Internet. Because of this, late last year we took a step that generated some considerable interest among libraries.

In September 1990, we provided free access to the Library of Congress machine-readable cataloging (LCMARC) database to all institutions, worldwide, on the Internet. That step caused many to stop and take

---

*This paper summarizes comments made by the author as part of a panel discussion titled "The Role of Traditional Library Networks."

notice. My phone rang frequently, followed by the question, "Why are you doing that—why aren't you charging for this service?" My answer was because it was an experiment—an experiment designed to see what kind of demand there was and what else was needed to support the database.

Although access was limited, we have seen anywhere from a high of 1,000 searches a month to a low of 700. Access has been from the United States, Canada, Japan, Australia, Germany, France, Norway, and Sweden—although my personal favorite was when the Library of Congress logged in to look at their own database! Wondering if the international viewing of full MARC records was piquing their interest, we were inclined to contact our lawyers and begin preparing our defense. Alas, such action has not been necessary.

NETWORKS' EFFECT ON TRADITIONAL BIBLIOGRAPHIC SERVICES

This experiment has certainly provided us with some interesting observations about how networks will affect the so-called "traditional bibliographic services." Specifically, we see the following needs emerging:

1. Traditional search capabilities will not be adequate. The user will want and demand a comprehensive range of search keys as well as expanded and consistent indexing. Although these may seem obvious and even self-evident, we must remember that the users accessing these databases will come far beyond the reach of our logic, training, or documentation. The search capability must pay attention to this fact.

2. Specialization of databases will become a natural outgrowth of networking. This specialization will not be related just to database content but also to the packaging of the information. Integrating the information with graphics, images, and sound will be a major means of differentiation. Database providers (library or vendors) should also specialize in the areas of database expertise and management to provide a further level of specialization. This will help eliminate the duplication of resources that exists on the networks—duplication that results in waste and confusion. Furthermore, this kind of specialization would be a natural outgrowth of cooperative collection development.

3. Until such specialization occurs—undoubtedly something that will take a very long time—we must begin to develop as part of our search capabilities semi-intelligent software that will interrogate the network without constant user interaction. It is absurd for us to expect end-users to navigate the network and to learn the different search

commands and database content. If we do that, users will quickly tire of the mechanisms currently in place and will underutilize the network resource.

4. Implementation and support of standards will help address this problem. Services that do not support Z39.50 and interfaces that do not support Z39.58 will face a slow and painful death. Rather than spending time developing terminal emulation packages, we should devote those resources to the implementation of standards so that the communication is at the process level—where it belongs. Then it will not matter what terminal is used or what interface. Furthermore, one must become involved in the standards process. Those who are not members of National Information Standards Organization (NISO) should be. Standards are the key to networking.

5. Cooperation between utilities is also becoming important. The ability of users to move easily between databases dictates not only the standards compliance just mentioned, but also the entire range of mechanisms that supports easy, transparent, and effective movement.

6. Interlibrary loan (ILL) processes should be revised. The opening of these databases across networks dictates that ILL, the process that has come to be known largely as a backroom behemoth, is not adequate. ILL now moves to the forefront and becomes a user option that must be easily invoked and readily served.

7. Closely coupled to ILL is the need to support delivery processes such as FAX, full-text delivery, and photocopying, particularly with regard to journal articles. Access to the databases on the network only proves that we can help the user quickly identify the work they need—but if we then make the user wait for days or weeks for delivery, we have failed. We must begin moving quickly to ensure that once the work is identified via the network, we use that same network to ensure prompt delivery.

8. We must also deal with all these costs and the need for increased demands on our computing resources. For a business such as Data Research Associates, this is, of course, easy. We charge for the services provided. Many will seek to do this by restriction of access, using policies that are in their own way the very equivalent of charging. Many of you have said, "We can't afford to do this," but isn't that the same as denying access? In that context, access with charge structures should be examined. These structures should compensate the library adequately for also providing access to those who are less technically and financially capable. But the fact remains that one must learn how to charge for services.

It is not acceptable to simply take a budget cut—one must look for ways to recover that lost revenue, for example, by offering library training as a mandatory course with credit-hour charges being credited to the library like any other department. If we can charge laboratory fees to make sure we have microscopes, why can't we charge library fees to make sure we have books? If we can charge for photocopies, why can't we charge for computer printouts? Understanding that these things always cost money—is it just a matter of do we do indirect billing or direct billing? If we continue to rely on indirect billing, we leave ourselves open to budget cuts because it is much harder to link indirect costs directly to service provided. A direct charge is in one's best long-term interests. What we really need now is entrepreneurial librarians.

9. We also wonder if we are placing too much hope on the National Research and Education Network (NREN) and if we are overlooking an obvious network that is already in place—OCLC. Should we not consider having OCLC enhance the network services and connect to NREN as a subnet?

CONCLUSION

Answers to these needs are not going to come easily. Although the needs may be rather easily described, the solutions require steps that do not come naturally to libraries. The desire to own materials, to limit access to one's immediate constituency, not to charge for services, and not to cooperate all come as a longstanding tradition in this field. Yet networking isn't paying attention to those traditions; it is forcing us to cooperate or be bypassed.

As providers of an information network, Data Research is paying attention to these needs. Enhanced search capabilities are being implemented on our databases—capabilities that recognize that these databases will be accessed via the Internet, Tymnet, and DRANET and by people who are not necessarily librarians and who do not have a librarian anywhere nearby. We are working on software that automatically interrogates multiple databases for the user. Although we originally mounted a rather traditional database, LCMARC, we are now specializing and mounting databases like the LC authority files in order to support networked authority verification, full-text files that support document delivery, and imaging support.

The issue of pricing is an area where we are making tremendous headway through our partnership with Information Access Co. (IAC). We are offering fixed-rate pricing for citation databases and will soon be offering site licensing of full-text databases. Of course, we have long been known for our ardent advocacy of standards implementation, and we continue that course. We understand that cooperation between

networks and, indeed, the very ability to network are absolutely
contingent on standards. We are moving ahead on all of these needs
and more because we believe that the networks are the access mechanism
for the libraries of tomorrow.

BRETT SUTTON

Assistant Professor
Graduate School of Library and Information Science
University of Illinois at Urbana-Champaign

Libraries and Networked Information Systems: Selected Bibliography

This bibliography is intended to suggest background reading on the origins and emerging uses of electronic networks by libraries and higher education. It is not the purpose of this list to provide an exhaustive or comprehensive set of references in so wide-ranging and rapidly evolving a field as networking. The list does not focus, for example, on the technology of networking, local area networks, specific software applications, or the commercial aspects of networking, although all of these subjects are touched on occasionally in the sources cited here. The best source of current information about library networking is the Internet itself. Interested readers with network access who are willing to do some browsing will discover a variety of relevant and continuously updated discussion groups, electronic journals, information servers, and document archives devoted to these topics.

Adams, R. J. (1990). *Communication and delivery systems for librarians.* Aldershot, England: Gower.

Arms, C. (Ed.). (1988). *Campus networking strategies.* Bedford, MA: Digital Press.

Arms, C. (Ed.). (1990). *Campus strategies for libraries and electronic information.* Bedford, MA: Digital Press.

Arms, C. R. (1990). A new information infrastructure. *Online, 14*(5), 15-22.

Arms, C. R. (1990). Using the national networks: BITNET and the Internet. *Online, 14*(5), 24-29.

Avram, H. D. (1987). Toward a nationwide library network. *Journal of Library Administration, 8*(3/4), 95-115.

Avram, H. D. (1988). Building a unified information network. *Library Hi Tech, 6*(4), 117-119.

Avram, H. D. (1989). Copyright in the electronic environment. *EDUCOM Review, 24*(3), 31-33.

Bailey, C. W., Jr. (1991). Electronic (online) publishing in action...The public-access computer systems review and other electronic serials. *Online, 15*(1), 28-35.

Bailey, C. W., Jr. (1991). Electronic serials on BITNET. *Computers in Libraries, 11*(4), 50.

Bell, G. C. (1988). Gordon Bell calls for a U.S. research network. *IEEE Spectrum, 25*(2), 54-57.

Bell, G. C. (1988). Steps toward a national research telecommunications network. *Library Hi Tech, 6*(1), 33-36.

Bloch, E. (1988). A national network: Today's reality, tomorrow's vision, part 1. *EDUCOM Bulletin, 23*(2/3), 11-13.

Brevik, P. S., & Shaw, W. (1989). Libraries prepare for an information age. *Educational Record, 70*(1), 12-19.

Britten, W. A. (1990). BITNET and the Internet: Scholarly networks for librarians. *College & Research Library News, 51*(2), 103-107.

Buckland, M. K., & Lynch, C. A. (1987). The Linked Systems Protocol and the future of bibliographic networks and systems. *Information Technology and Libraries, 6*(2), 83-88.

Catlett, C. E. (1989). The NSFNET: Beginnings of a national research internet. *Academic Computing, 3*(5), 18-21.

Cline, N. (1990). Information resources and the national network. *EDUCOM Review, 25*(2), 30-34.

Communications, Computers and Networks. (1991). [Special Issue]. *Scientific American, 265*(3).

Denenberg, R. (1990). Data communications and OSI. *Library Hi Tech, 8*(4), 15-32.

Fenly, J. G., & Wiggins, B. (1988). *The Linked Systems Project: A networking tool for librarians.* Dublin, OH: OCLC.

Gore, A. (1990). Remarks on the NREN. *EDUCOM Review, 25*(2), 12-16.

Gould, C. C. (Ed.). (1989). *The information web: Ethical and social implications of computer networking.* Boulder, CO: Westview Press.

Hall, S. C. (1991). The four stages of National Research and Education Network growth. *EDUCOM Review, 26*(1), 18-24.

Henry, M.; Keenan, L.; & Reagan, M. (1991). *Search sheets for OPACs on the Internet, 1992.* Westport, CT: Meckler.

Hildreth, C. R. (1987). *Library automation in North America: A reassessment of the impact of new technologies on networking.* Munich: K. G. Saur.

Holligan, P. J. (1986). *Access to academic networks.* London: Taylor Graham.

Inter-University Committee on Computing and Standing Conference of National and University Libraries Information Services Working Party. (1990). Computer-based information services in universities. *British Journal of Academic Librarianship, 5*(1), 1-30.

Kahn, R. E. (1988). A national network: Today's reality, tomorrow's vision, part 2. *EDUCOM Bulletin, 23*(2/3), 14-21.

Kalin, S. W., & Tennant, R. (1991). Beyond OPACs...the wealth of information resources on the Internet. *Database, 14*(4), 28-33.

Kibbey, M., & Evans, N. H. (1989). The network is the library. *EDUCOM Review, 24*(3), 15-20.

LaQuey, T. L. (1989). Networks for academics. *Academic Computing, 4*(3), 32-39.

LaQuey, T. L. (Ed.). (1990). *The user's directory of computer networks.* Bedford, MA: Digital Press.

Learn, L. L. (1988). Networks: The telecommunications infrastructure and impacts of change. *Library Hi Tech, 6*(1), 13-31.

Lynch, C. A. (1989). Library automation and the national research network. *EDUCOM Review, 24*(3), 21-26.

Lynch, C. A. (1989). Linking library automation systems to the Internet: Functional requirements, planning, and policy issues. *Library Hi Tech, 7*(4), 7-18.

Lynch, C. A. (1990). Information retrieval as a network application. *Library Hi Tech, 8*(4), 57-72.

Lynch, C. A., & Preston, C. M. (1990). Internet access to information resources. In M. E. Williams (Ed.), *Annual review of information science and technology* (Vol. 25, pp. 263-312). Amsterdam: Elsevier Science.

Lynch, C. A., & Preston, C. M. (1991). Evolution of networked information sources. In M. E. Williams (Ed.), *12th National Online Meeting Proceedings* (pp. 221-230). Medford, NJ: Learned Information.

McClure, C. R. (Ed.). (1991). *The National Research and Education Network (NREN): Research and policy perspectives.* New York: Ablex.

McGill, M. J. (1989). Z39.50 benefits for designers and users. *EDUCOM Review, 24*(3), 27-30.

Mitchell, M. M., & Saunders, L. M. (1991). The virtual library: An agenda for the 1990s. *Computers in Libraries, 11*(4), 8-11.

Neubauer, K. W., & Dyer, E. R. (Eds.). (1990). *European library networks.* Norwood, NJ: Ablex.

Nielsen, B. (1990). PC monitor—Finding it on the Internet: The next challenge for librarianship. *Database, 13*(5), 105-107.

Osburn, C. B. (1989). The structuring of the scholarly communication system. *College & Research Libraries, 50*(3), 277-286.

Palca, J. (1990). BITNET headed for new frontiers. *Science, 247*(4042), 520.

Palca, J. (1991). New journal will publish without paper. *Science, 253*(5027), 1480.

Parkhurst, C. A. (Ed.). (1990). *Library perspectives on NREN: The National Research and Education Network.* Chicago: Library and Information Technology Association.

Quarterman, J. S. (1990). *The matrix: Computer networks and conferencing systems worldwide.* Bedford, MA: Digital Press.

Schultz, B. (1988). The evolution of ARPANET. *Datamation, 34*(15), 71-74.

Schuyler, M. (1990). *Dial in: 1990-1991. An annual guide to library online public access catalogs in North America.* Westport, CT: Meckler.

Sloan, B. G. (1990). *Linked systems for resource sharing.* Boston: G. K. Hall.

Slonim, J., & Bauer, M. A. (1990). The information utility project: Glimpse into the library of the future. *Information Processing & Management, 26*(4), 467-488.

Strangelove, M., & Kovacs, D. (Comps). (1991). *Directory of electronic journals, newsletters and academic discussion lists.* Washington, DC: Association of Research Libraries.

Sugnet, C. (Ed.). (1988). Networking in transition: Current and future issues. *Library Hi Tech, 6*(4), 101-119.

Van Houweling, D. E. (1989). The national network: A national interest. *EDUCOM Review, 24*(2), 14-18.

Weingarten, F. (1991). Five steps to NREN enlightenment. *EDUCOM Review, 26*(1), 26-30.

Williams, B. (1991). *A directory of computer conferencing for libraries.* Westport, CT: Meckler.

Woodsworth, A., & Wall, T. B. (1991). *Understanding library cooperation and networks: A basic reader.* New York: Neal-Schuman.

Wright, K. (1990). The road to the global village. *Scientific American, 262*(3), 83-85.

CONTRIBUTORS

CHARLES E. CATLETT is Manager of Networking Development at the National Center for Supercomputing Applications (NCSA), located at the University of Illinois at Urbana-Champaign. He is principal investigator for NCSA's work developing applications and programming environments for the BLANCA gigabit-per-second network testbed, one of five such testbeds being coordinated by the Corporation for National Research Initiatives with funding from industry, the National Science Foundation, and the Defense Advanced Research Projects Agency. The Networking Development group at NCSA is currently involved in gigabit applications, high-performance mass storage archives, wide area network needs analysis, and local area gigabit LANs. The scientific multimedia digital library is one of several applications being developed in Mr. Catlett's group for use on the BLANCA gigabit-per-second network testbed. Mr. Catlett received a B.S. in Computer Engineering from the University of Illinois at Urbana-Champaign, in 1983.

CHARLES H. DAVIS is Professor of Library and Information Science at the University of Illinois at Urbana-Champaign, where he was also Dean from 1979 to 1986. Before coming to Illinois, he was Professor and Dean of the faculty of Library Science at the University of Alberta in Edmonton, Canada; he also taught at the University of Michigan and Drexel University. A chemist as well as an information scientist and librarian, Dr. Davis worked as an index editor for the Chemical Abstracts Service before entering academic life. He is a principal author of several books, including *Guide to Information Science* and *Pascal Programming for Libraries*. His research interests include computer-based retrieval techniques and interface design. He currently enjoys an appointment as Visiting Scholar at Indiana University in Bloomington, Indiana, where he resides with his wife, her dog, and his cat.

CARL GRANT is Vice President of Marketing at Data Research Associates. He began at Data Research in 1984 as a Consultant and has held a variety of management positions within the company.

Previous to working for Data Research, he spent thirteen years in libraries where he implemented and managed library automation systems. Mr. Grant has an M.L.S. from the University of Missouri and is a participant in ALA, LITA, NISO, AVIAC, and CNI activities.

KENNETH R. R. GROS LOUIS is Professor of English and Comparative Literature at Indiana University and is Vice President of Indiana University and Chancellor of the Bloomington campus. He has served since 1986 as Chairman of the Committee on Institutional Cooperation and has been a member of the Commission on Preservation and Access since 1986. In addition, he has served as a member and Chair of the Board of Directors of the Center for Research Libraries.

M. E. L. JACOB is a writer, consultant, and publisher of *Entrak*. She teaches workshops in strategic planning and library networking. Ms. Jacob is active in a number of library and information science associations and societies and is a frequent speaker at conferences. She has worked at OCLC and in university, public, and special libraries.

CLIFFORD LYNCH is the Director of the Division of Library Automation at the University of California Office of the President, where he is responsible for the MELVYL® information system, one of the largest public access information retrieval systems in existence, as well as the computer internetwork linking the nine UC campuses. He has been at the University of California in various positions since 1979. Dr. Lynch has also been involved in a wide variety of research and development efforts in the application of advanced technologies to information management and delivery, including work with computer networking, information servers, database management systems, and imaging technologies. Dr. Lynch received his Ph.D. in Computer Science from the University of California at Berkeley. He participates in several standards activities (including the NISO Standards Development Committee), is Principal Investigator of various research grants, and is the author of several books and over fifty published papers.

SUSAN K. MARTIN is University Librarian at Georgetown University. She received her Ph.D. in Library and Information Studies from the University of California, Berkeley. She has been active in library automation and networking since 1964 and has most recently become involved in an effort to define a strategic vision for librarianship.

PAUL EVAN PETERS is Director of the Coalition for Networked Information, a joint project of the Association of Research Libraries, CAUSE, and EDUCOM that promotes creation of and access to information resources in networked environments in order to enrich scholarship and to enhance intellectual productivity. Before founding the Coalition in March 1990, Mr. Peters was Systems Coordinator at the New York Public Library from 1987 through 1989, and was Assistant University Librarian for Systems at Columbia University, where he also earned a masters degree in sociology, from 1979 through 1986. Mr. Peters holds a masters degree in library and information sciences from the University of Pittsburgh and, as an undergraduate, studied computer science and philosophy at the University of Dayton. Mr. Peters is currently President of the Library and Information Technology Association, is past-Chair of the National Information Standards Organization, and serves on the editorial boards of *Library Hi Tech* and *Public Access Computer Systems Review.*

MARTIN RUNKLE is Director of the University of Chicago Library.

JAMES E. RUSH is Executive Director of PALINET. He is also current Chair of the Regional OCLC Network Directors Advisory Committee (RONDAC) and serves as Chair of the Board of Directors of the National Information Standards Organization (NISO). Prior to joining PALINET in 1988, Dr. Rush was president of a consulting firm, and he continues to consult with libraries and information centers on automation through PALINET. Rush has a B.S. in Chemistry and Mathematics from Central Missouri State University and a Ph.D. in Organic Chemistry from the University of Missouri (Columbia). He is the coauthor (with Charles H. Davis) of two books on information science, has written extensively on computer, library, and information science, and is the editor of an eight-volume set of Library Systems Evaluation Guides and of a looseleaf update service Microcomputers for Libraries: Product Review and Procurement Guide (both published by his consulting firm).

THOMAS W. SHAUGHNESSY is University Librarian at the University of Minnesota's Twin City Campus. He received his Ph.D. from Rutgers University. He has published articles on a variety of administrative issues and is active in the Association of Research Libraries and the American Library Association.

WILLIAM J. STUDER has been Director of Libraries at The Ohio State University since 1977. He holds the B.A., M.A., and Ph.D. degrees from Indiana University (the latter two in library/information science). He has given and published papers on a variety of library management and economy issues.

BRETT SUTTON is on the faculty of the Graduate School of Library and Information Science at the University of Illinois, Urbana-Champaign. He holds a Ph.D. in Anthropology and an M.S. in Library Science from the University of North Carolina, Chapel Hill. His areas of interest include the sociology of knowledge, libraries and society, social science information sources, and information technology.

JEFFREY TERSTRIEP is Project Leader in the Networking Development group at the National Center for Supercomputing Applications (NCSA) at the University of Illinois, Urbana-Champaign. He holds a B.S. in Electrical Engineering from the University of Illinois at Urbana-Champaign. Presently, he is spearheading the effort to develop distributed applications on the BLANCA testbed, one of five national wide area gigabit networks. In addition, he is the architect of the Data Management Facility. He also teaches two courses at the community college: Beginning Computer Graphics and Scientific Visualization.

INDEX

Prepared by Laurel Preece

Abstracting and indexing (A&I) databases: electronic access to, 21, 107; and personal scholarly publishing, 28-29

Academic libraries: impact of electronic networks on, 30-32. *See also* Research libraries

Academic Strategy, 125, 127

Acquisitions: costs of library materials, 53-56; effect of electronic networks on, 34

Adams, R. J., 137

Advanced Networks and Services (ANS): and the National Research and Education Network, 63; and SONET-level services, 16

Advanced Research Project Agency: and the ARPANET, 3, 15, 47

Advanced Technology Group. *See* Apple Computer Library

American Association for the Advancement of Science: and electronic publishing, 7

American Chemical Society: and electronic information distribution, 24

American Library Association (ALA). Library and Information Technology Association: and electronic networks, 9

American Physics Society: and electronic information distribution, 24

ANS. *See* Advanced Networks and Services

Apple Computer Library: and networking applications, 101

Apple Macintosh (computer): and network access packages, 87

Archie FTP: access to archives on electronic networks, 21

Archival function of libraries: effect of electronic networks on, 34

Archives, electronic: 7; on the Internet, 86-87

ARL. *See* Association of Research Libraries

ARL Statistics, 1983-84, 107

ARL Statistics, 1989-90, 105

Arms, C. R., 137, 138

ARPANET, 3, 15, 20

Association of Research Libraries (ARL): and the Coalition for Networked Information, 58; costs of library materials, 53-54; interlibrary loan statistics, 125, 126

ATLAS system (Data Research Associates Inc.): and the virtual library concept, 76

Avram, H. D., 138

Bailey, C. W., Jr., 138

Battin, P., 76, 82

Bauer, M. A., 140

Behold Metatron: The Recording Angel, 30

Bell, G. C., 138

Berger, M. G., 25, 38

BIMA (Berkeley-Illinois-Maryland Array): and digital access, 87, 89, 94

BISDN (Broadband Integrated Services Digital Network): transmission speeds, 17

BITNET, 3, 41, 71, 72; and electronic mail, 14; and evolution of the National Research and Education Network, 66

Bloch, E., 138

Brevik, P. S., 138

Brin, David, 26, 38

Britten, W. A., 138

Broadband Integrated Services Digital Network (BISDN): transmission speeds, 17

Brown, Rowland, 125

Brownrigg, E. B., 15, 39

BRS: and electronic networks, 4, 22; and the National Research and Education Network, 69; workstation software and ILLINET Online, 103

Buckland, Michael K., 25, 37, 38, 138

Bulletin boards. *See* Electronic bulletin boards

Business and industry. *See* Private sector

CALL (Computer Access Linking Libraries): interface with PREPnet, 79, 80

Campus-wide information systems (CWISs): and electronic networks, 21, 51

CARL (Colorado Alliance of Research Libraries), 102; and book reviews from *Choice*, 7; and the virtual library concept, 76

CARL Systems, 102

Carnegie-Mellon University: and the virtual library concept, 76; electronic mail and online catalog users at, 103

Catalogs, online: access on the Internet, 68-69; and electronic networks, 51; and library networking, 6; and the ideal library, 110; at the University of Chicago, 105, 106-107

Catlett, Charles E., 6, 77, 82, 84, 85, 98, 138, 141

CAUSE: and the Coalition for Networked Information, 58

CD-ROM (Compact Disc-Read Only Memory): bibliographies and indexes, 111, 114; effect on library local area networks, 4; effect on resource sharing, 125; the University of Alaska oral history project, 101

Center for Research Libraries, 119

Chernow, R., 36, 38

CIC (Committee on Institutional Cooperation), 11, 119, 120, 121

CICNet, 11; and electronic networks, 9; and library catalog search systems, 85-86

Cisler, Steve, 11, 101, 103

Clark, Roger, 11

Cline, N., 138

CM-2: and multimedia digital library applications, 94, 95, 96, 97

Coalition for Networked Information: and electronic networks, 9, 58, 61; and the National Research and Education Network, 70-71, 72, 78

Colorado Alliance of Research Libraries. *See* CARL

Commission on Preservation and Access, 119

Committee on Institutional Cooperation (CIC), 11, 119, 120, 121

Common carriers: and electronic networks, 16

Communication: and the role of the librarian, 99-100

"Communications, Computers and Networks," 138

Competitive intelligence: and electronic networks, 25-27

CompuServe, 14, 68

Computer Access Linking Libraries. *See* CALL

Computer conferences. *See* Electronic conferences

Conferences. *See* Electronic conferences

Connectivity, 14-20, 41-42, 103; costs, 130-131; international communications links, 16

Copyright: and electronic networks, 19, 102; and multimedia, 27; and personal scholarly publishing, 28

Costs: of archiving electronic data, 129; of computer printer paper, 131; of connectivity, 130-131; of interlibrary loan, 115-116, 125-126, 130; of Internet access, 131; of library materials, 53-56; of library networking, 118-122, 123-127, 128-131; of maintaining dual collections, 129, 131; of networked resources compared with print resources, 55-56; of training, 129

Council on Library Resources: and the economics of research libraries, 104

CRAY Y-MP (computer): and multimedia digital library applications, 94, 95, 97

Cryptographic technologies: and electronic networks, 20
Cummings, Martin M., 104, 113, 117
Current Cites, 35
CWIS. *See* Campus-wide information systems
Cybernautics: and electronic networks, 53

DARPA. *See* Defense Advanced Research Projects Agency
Dartmouth College: and the Shakespeare database, 7; and the virtual library concept, 76
Data Research Associates, 132, 134
Daval, N., 107, 117
Davis, Charles H., 38, 120, 141
DBIL. *See* Distributed Biomedical Imaging Laboratory
Defense Advanced Research Projects Agency (DARPA): and gigabits-persecond testbeds, 16
DeGennaro, Dick, 124
Denenberg, R., 138
Department of Defense: and the ARPANET, 3, 15, 47; and the Internet, 15; and the National Research and Education Network, 63
Department of Energy: and electronic networks, 47; and the National Research and Education Network, 62, 63
DIALOG: and electronic networks, 4, 22, 43; and the National Research and Education Network, 69; and the PALINET model for regional networking, 80; online databases, 6
Digital libraries, 51, 85-87; and networked information resources and services, 50-53. *See also* Multimedia digital libraries
Dillon, Martin, 11
Disintermediation: and electronic networks, 22-24
Distributed Biomedical Imaging Laboratory (DBIL): and multimedia digital library applications, 97
Dougan, W. L., 75, 82
Dougherty, R. M., 75, 82
Dowd, Sheila, 125
Dowlin, K. E., 33, 38
DRANET: 132-136

Dyer, E. R., 139

Earth, 26
Earth Observing System (EOS): and digital access, 87
EasyNet: and the PALINET model for regional networking, 80
Economics of Research Libraries, 104
EDUCOM: and the Coalition for Networked Information, 58; and the National Research and Education Network, 77
EDUCOM National NET'91. *See* National NET'91
EEC. *See* European Economic Community
Electronic bulletin boards, 129; access on the Internet, 86-87
Electronic conferences, 6, 50; and the National Research and Education Network, 68
Electronic Frontier Foundation: and electronic networks, 9
Electronic mail, 6, 50; and the ARPANET, 20; and the BITNET, 14; and CompuServe, 14; and the Internet, 14, 20; and MCIMAIL, 14; and the National Research and Education Network, 68; and the PALINET model for regional networking, 79, 80; and USENET, 14; at Carnegie-Mellon University, 103; network billing algorithms, 92-93
Electronic networks. *See* Networks, electronic
Electronic publishing, 7, 50, 56, 129, 131. *See also* Personal scholarly publishing
End-user workstations, 24-29
Environmental Protection Agency: and the National Research and Education Network, 63
EPIC Service (OCLC): and the PALINET model for regional networking, 80
Ethical aspects of networks: 8, 30-34
European Economic Community (EEC): and the establishment of international networks, 17
Evans, N. H., 139

Fast Fourier Transform. *See* FFT

Faxon Institute conference: and computer conferencing, 68
FCCSET (Federal Computer Council for Science, Energy, and Technology): and the National Research and Education Network, 63
Federal Communications Commission (FCC): and spectrum support for public wireless data communications, 15-16
Federal Computer Council for Science, Energy, and Technology. *See* FCCSET
Federal Networking Council: and the National Research and Education Network, 63
Fenly, J. G., 138
FFT (Fast Fourier Transform): and multimedia digital library applications, 93
FIDONET, 5
File transfer protocol (FTP): and access to electronic archives, 20, 21, 86-87
FreeNet, 7
FTP. *See* File transfer protocol; Archie FTP

Getty Art History Information Program: access to multimedia resources, 27-28
Getz, M., 77, 82
Gibson, William, 14, 38
Gore, Albert, Jr., 3, 15, 49, 61, 62, 138
Gould, C. C., 138
Grant, Carl R., 11, 132, 141
Green, Harold, 17
Gros Louis, Kenneth R. R., 118, 123, 128, 142
Gusack, Nancy, 38

Haas, J. Warren, 117
Hall, S. C., 138
Hat Creek radio telescope: and multimedia digital library applications, 89, 93-94
Health and medical information: access at public libraries, 33
Henry, M., 138
High-Performance Computing Act of 1991: and the National Research and Education Network, 3, 63-64
High-Performance Computing and Communications Initiative, 15

High-volume print facilities: and electronic networks, 51-52
Hildreth, C. R., 139
Holligan, P. J., 139
Hubble Space Telescope: and digital access, 87
Human Genome Project: and digital access, 87
Hunt, Paul M., 11, 118, 123, 128

IAC. *See* Information Access Co.
IBM: and Advanced Networks and Services, 16, 63; and electronic networks, 47
ILCSO, 103
ILL. *See* Interlibrary loan
ILLINET (Illinois Library Network) Online, 103
Illinois Library Computer Systems Office (ILCSO), 103
INCOLSA (Indiana Cooperative Library Services Authority): proposal for a multilevel national network, 76-77
Indiana University, 119
Information Access Co., 103, 135
Information and Information Systems, 37
Information technology and libraries. *See* Networks, electronic
Innes, H. A., 13, 38
Integrated Services Digital Network (ISDN): transmission speeds, 17
Intelligent databases: and electronic networks, 52-53
Inter-University Committee on Computing and Standing Conference of National and University Libraries Information Services Working Party, 139
Interlibrary loan, 31, 115-116, 125-126, 130, 134
Internet, 5, 21, 41; access issues, 10, 131; and CARL online systems, 102; and data havens, 19; and Data Research databases, 135; and digital libraries, 85-87; and DRANET, 132; and electronic mail, 14, 20; and government networks, 15; and ILLINET Online, 103; and K-12 institutional connectivity, 85; and library catalogs, 51; and the National Research and Education

Network, 66, 67; and OPACs, 128-129; and PREPnet, 79; and remote access, 91-93; and the University of Chicago, 105; archive access, 86-87; connectivity, 14; control issues, 9; cost structure, 93; growth of, 3, 4, 84-85, 86; transmission speeds, 16
ISDN (Integrated Services Digital Network): transmission speeds, 17

Jacob, M. E. L., 99, 142
Johns Hopkins University: and the Knowledge Management process, 35

Kahn, R. E., 139
Kalin, S. W., 139
Keenan, L., 138
Keller, George, 125, 127
Kibbey, M., 139
Kilgour, Frederick, G., 75, 82
"Knowbots": and electronic networks, 52-53
Knowledge Management process, 35
Koenig, M. E. D., 75, 82
Kovacs, D., 140
Kuttner, R., 18, 38

LaQuey, T. L., 139
Larsen, Ron, 43, 44, 45
Lawrence Berkeley Laboratories: multimedia digital library applications, 97
LCMARC database: access through DRANET, 132-133, 135
Leadership: librarians and information technology, 111-112; librarians and the National Research and Education Network, 71-72
Learn, L. L., 139
Legal aspects of electronic networks, 8, 19. *See also* Copyright
Lehigh University: and the virtual library concept, 76
LEXIS, 22, 43, 114
Library and Information Technology Association: and electronic networks, 9
Library networking. *See* Networks, electronic
Library of Congress, 25, 38; and the National Research and Education Network, 63

Library of Congress machine-readable cataloging. *See* LCMARC
Library of Congress Network Advisory Committee: and a proposal for a multilevel national network, 77
Library schools: and electronic networks, 36-38
Lichtenstein, A., 107, 117
Likins, Peter, 66, 73, 77, 78, 82
LISTSERV software: and computer conferencing, 3
Listservers, 129
Local area networks: access to online catalogs, 101-102; at the University of Chicago, 105; NSFNET architecture, 85
Loken, S. C., 24, 38
Lombardi, J. T., 75, 82
Lucier, R. E., 35, 38
Lucky, R. W., 26, 38
Lynch, Clifford A., 5, 12, 15, 22, 25, 38, 39, 101, 138, 139, 142

Machine-readable cataloging. *See* MARC
Macintosh computers: and network access packages, 87
MARC: and library networking, 4
Martin, Susan K., 142
Massachusetts Institute of Technology: Project INTREX, 103
McAdams, A. K., 75, 82
McClure, C. R., 139
McGill, M. J., 139
MCI: and Advanced Networks and Services, 16; and electronic networks, 47; and the National Research and Education Network, 63
MCIMAIL, 14
MEDLINE: and access to health and medical information at public libraries, 33
MELVYL system, 6
Merit: and the National Research and Education Network, 63
MILNET, 15
MIT: Project INTREX, 103
Mitchell, M. M., 139
Molholt, P., 76, 82
Multimedia: and electronic networks, 27-28; impact on elementary schools and high schools, 27

Multimedia digital libraries: access to
data, 89-93; and electronic networks, 84-98; and the Internet, 85-
87; atmospheric sciences application, 94-97; biomedical imaging application, 97-98; contents of,
87-89; data storage, 89; directory
services, 89-90; National Center for
Supercomputing Applications
prototype, 89-98; network architectures and protocols, 90-93;
radio astronomy application, 93-94

National Aeronautics and Space Ad-
ministration (NASA): and electron-
ic networks, 47; and the Internet,
15; and the National Research and
Education Network, 63
National Agricultural Library (NAL):
and the National Research and
Education Network, 63; text-
digitizing project, 101
National Center for Supercomputing
Applications (NCSA): and multimedia digital libraries, 7, 84-98
National Information Standards Organization (NISO), 134
National Library of Medicine (NLM):
and the National Research and
Education Network, 63
National NET'91: and the National
Research and Education Network,
61, 66, 77; digital library dem-
onstration, 90, 91
National Research and Education
Network (NREN), 41, 61-73, 135;
access, 67-70; access costs, 65-66, 70-
71, 131; and computer conferencing,
68; and electronic mail, 68; and
electronic publishing, 129; and
library networking, 3-4; and
National NET'91, 77; and OCLC,
68; and RLG, 68; and the Coalition
for Networked Information, 78;
capacity of, 3; connectivity issues,
14-15; evolution of, 66; governance
structure, 62-64; leadership roles, 71-
72; legislation, 62-64; role of for-
profit organizations in network
development, 65; role of librarians
in network development, 64-65;
school and library connectivity, 64-
65; scope and benefits, 77-78

National Science Foundation (NSF):
and electronic networks, 47; and
gigabits-per-second testbeds, 16;
and the Internet, 15; and the
National Research and Education
Network, 3, 63; and the NSFNET,
41, 85
NCSA. See National Center for Supercomputing Applications
Neal, Jim, 120, 122
Network File System (NFS [Sun Mi-
crosystems]): and remote access to
data, 91-92
Networked information resources and
services. See Networks, electronic
Networks, electronic: advanced, 41-48;
authorization and resource control,
102; bibliography, 137-140; budgeting for library networking, 120-121;
cooperation and library networking, 121-122; database search capabilities, 133; delivery processes,
134; development of new marketplaces, 18, 57-58; development of
the information refiner, 29-30;
directories to resources, 102; effect
on traditional bibliographic
services, 133-135; ethical aspects, 8,
30-34; governance issues, 62-64, 119-
120; information utilities, 22; international communications monopolies, 16; legal considerations,
8, 19; metaphors for networking
technology, 48-50; multimedia, 27-
28; origins, 3-5, 66; performance
levels, 44-47; politics of, 127;
proposal for a multilevel national
network, 76-77; public rights versus
property rights, 100; repercussions
of data availability, 26; reporting
lines and library networking, 122;
research and education networks,
47-48; resource sharing and library
networking, 124-126; resources and
services, 20-24, 40-60, 128-130;
service to the private sector, 74-83;
specialization of databases, 133;
standards, 4, 6, 134; system boundaries, 100; training of information
professionals, 36-38; transmission
speeds, 17, 44-47; user interfaces,
134. See also Academic libraries;
ARPANET; BITNET; Connectiv-

ity; Costs; Internet; MILNET; National Research and Education Network; NSFNET; Public libraries; Research libraries; Special libraries
Neubauer, K. W., 139
NEXIS: 114
NeXT: multimedia mail system, 27
NFS. *See* Network File System
Nielsen, B., 140
NISO (National Information Standards Organization), 134
North Carolina State University: text-digitizing project, 101
NREN. *See* National Research and Education Network
NSFNET, 3, 41; access to high-end specialized equipment, 20; architecture, 85; electronic mail, 50; evolution of the National Research and Education Network, 66, 68; growth of connectivity, 42; performance levels, 44-47; transmission speeds, 16

OCLC, 4, 43, 135; and electronic publishing, 7; and the Internet, 51; and the National Research and Education Network, 68; and the proposal for a multilevel national network, 77, 81; and the virtual library concept, 123
Office of Management and Budget: and the National Research and Education Network, 63
Office of Science and Technology Planning: and the National Research and Education Network, 15
Office of Science and Technology Policy: and the National Research and Education Network, 63
Office of Technology Assessment, 18, 19, 39
Ohio State University Libraries: interlibrary loan, 130
Online Journal of Current Clinical Trials, 7
OPACs (online public access catalogs), 4, 6; and interlibrary loan, 130; and resource sharing, 125; and the Internet, 128-129; and the virtual library concept, 124
Osburn, C. B., 140

Palca, J., 140
PALINET (Pennsylvania Area Library Network): model for regional planning with emphasis on the private sector, 76, 78-81
PALS (Project for Automated Library System [Unisys Corp.]): and the virtual library concept, 76
Paperwork Reduction Act, 71
Parkhurst, C. A., 140
Pennsylvania Area Library Network. *See* PALINET
Pennsylvania Research and Economic Partnership network. *See* PREPnet
Penrod, Jim, 127
Personal scholarly publishing, 7, 28-29
Peters, Paul Evan, 5, 17, 40, 142
Pfaffenberger, B., 22, 39
Pikes Peak Library District: and the virtual library concept, 76
Point-of-sale (POS) technology: and electronic networks, 26
PREPnet (Pennsylvania Research and Economic Partnership network): interface with CALL, 79, 80
Preservation: and electronic networks, 8, 56
Preston, C. M., 22, 38, 39, 139
Private sector: and the library, 74-83; and the PALINET model for regional networking, 78-81
Project for Automated Library System. *See* PALS
Project INTREX: annotation of bibliographic records with notes, 103
Project Jukebox: oral history project on CD-ROM at the University of Alaska, 101
Public bulletin boards. *See* Electronic bulletin boards
Public libraries: impact of electronic networks on, 32-33
Public rights versus property rights: and electronic networks, 100

Quarterman, John S., 14, 39, 79, 82, 140

Reagan, M., 138
Reitmeier, Glenn, 88
Research libraries: characteristics of the ideal library, 109-110; criteria in

quality assessment, 126; economics of, 104-117; and electronic networks, 1-3; and electronic network leadership, 5; networking applications, 99-103; politics of library networking, 127; standards in quality assessment, 126
Research Libraries Group (RLG): and the Internet, 51; and the National Research and Education Network, 68; interlibrary loan statistics, 126
Research Libraries Information Network (RLIN), 4, 43; and the virtual library concept, 123-124
Resource sharing: and electronic networks, 115-116, 124-126. *See also* Interlibrary loan
Richards, Berry, 82
Richardson, E. C., 115, 117
RLG. *See* Research Libraries Group
RLIN. *See* Research Libraries Information Network
RS/6000 workstations: and multimedia digital library applications, 96
Runkle, Martin, 9, 104, 143
Rush, James E., 74, 76, 77, 82, 83, 143

Saunders, L. M., 139
Scholarly publishing. *See* Personal scholarly publishing
Schultz, B., 140
Schuyler, M., 140
Self-publishing. *See* Personal scholarly publishing
Senate Energy Committee: and the National Research and Education Network, 62, 63
Senate Labor and Education Committee: and the National Research and Education Network, 62
Senate Science and Technology Committee: and the National Research and Education Network, 63
Shakespeare database, 7
Shaughnessy, Thomas W., 118, 123, 128, 143
Shaw, Ward, 11, 102, 138
Simple mail transport protocol (SMTP): and electronic mail, 92-93
Sloan, Bernard G., 11, 103, 140
Slonim, J., 140
Smarr, L. L., 85, 98

SMDS (Switched Multi-Megabyte Data Services): and transmission speeds, 16-17
SMTP (simple mail transport protocol): and electronic mail, 92-93
Space requirements: and electronic networks, 53
Special libraries: impact of electronic networks on, 32
St. George, A., 21, 39
Standards: for information retrieval, 4, 6, 134
Sterling, Bruce, 19, 39
Strangelove, M., 140
Stubbs, Kendon, 105, 107, 117
Studer, William J., 118, 123, 128, 143
Sugnet, C., 140
Supercomputers: and networked information resources and services, 50
Sutton, Brett, 11, 38, 120, 137, 143
Switched Multi-Megabyte Data Services (SMDS): transmission speeds, 16-17
System boundaries: and electronic networks, 100

Tennant, R., 139
Terstriep, Jeffrey A., 6, 84, 144
Training, 36-38, 129
Tymnet, 135

UNCOVER: and the Internet, 102
UNCOVER II: and the Internet, 102
United States Congress. Office of Technology Assessment. *See* Office of Technology Assessment
University Microfilms: and ILLINET Online, 103
University of Alaska (Fairbanks): oral history project on CD-ROM, 101
University of California (Berkeley): Current Cites and new roles for libraries, 35
University of California (Los Angeles) film and television archives: access to multimedia resources, 27
University of California (Oakland): MELVYL system, 6; WAIS Station, 101
University of Chicago: access to online databases in the Law Library, 114; electronic networking at, 105-106
University of Illinois. Biomedical

Magnetic Resonance Laboratory: multimedia digital library applications, 97
University of Minnesota libraries: interlibrary loan at, 125
UNIX-to-UNIX copy protocol (UUCP): and electronic mail, 92-93
USENET, 5, 14

Van Houweling, D. E., 140
Vietorisz, T., 75, 82
Virtual library, 8, 9, 76, 81, 105, 123-124, 131
Voges, Mickie, 11

WAIS (Wide Area Information Server) Station: and storage of mixed media information, 101
Waldhart, Tom, 125, 127
Wall, T. B., 140
Weingarten, F., 140
WELL, 5
WESTLAW: ownership versus access, 114
Wetherbee, Lou, 11
White House Conference on Library and Information Services, 71
Wide Area Information Server. *See* WAIS
Wiggins, B., 138
Williams, B., 140
Wilson: online databases, 6, 103
Wireless communication: and network connectivity, 15-16
Woodsworth, A., 140
Workstations: and electronic networks, 24-29
Worldnet, 26
Wright, K., 140

Yurick, Sol, 30, 39

Z39.50, 6, 134